STORIES
OF
PADRE PIO

"We must be alert on the road to salvation. Only the fervent succeed in reaching it, never the tepid or those who sleep!"

—Padre Pio
(Page 53)

Padre Pio
Capuchin priest who bore the stigmata.
1887-1968

STORIES
OF
PADRE PIO

By
Madame Katharina Tangari

Translated from the Italian by
John Collorafi

"And I live, now not I; but Christ liveth in me."
—Galatians 2:20

TAN BOOKS AND PUBLISHERS, INC.
Rockford, Illinois 61105

Library of Congress Catalog Card No.: 96-60694

ISBN 0-89555-536-0

This book was originally published under the title: *Besuche bei Pater Pio* (Verlag Franz Reisinger, Wels/Oberösterreich). It was translated from German into Italian by the author. This English edition was translated by John Collorafi from the Italian *Il Messaggio di Padre Pio*.

Note on the translation: Because Padre Pio has died since this book was first published, much of what was originally written in the present tense has been changed to the past tense in this edition.

Printed and bound in the United States of America.

TAN BOOKS AND PUBLISHERS, INC.
P.O. Box 424
Rockford, Illinois 61105
1996

Dedicated to
Our Lady of Grace

CONTENTS

DECLARATION OF OBEDIENCE

INTRODUCTION

I first heard about Padre Pio during Lent of 1949; it was on my return trip from Austria, on the train from Vienna to Rome. When we reached Venice, some naval officers came into my compartment. One of them asked me, "Madame, are you a foreigner?" And without waiting for my response, he continued, "There are many beautiful things abroad, but what we have, the foreigners don't!" Because I could not figure out what the officer was referring to, I asked him to tell me, and he stated, with some solemnity:

"We have Padre Pio!"

Padre Pio? I had never heard this name before. The officer described for me some well-nigh miraculous events from Padre Pio's life. By now I was curious and asked who he was.

"He's a Capuchin Father," the officer answered, "who has borne the wounds of Jesus for years!"

The officers left at Bologne. I would have liked to know his address, but when I thought of asking where Padre Pio was, it was too late. The officer, who with such enthusiasm had told me about the Padre, did not have time to write his address, but he said, "You'll find Padre Pio. You'll certainly find him!"

As a matter of fact, I did not try to find Padre Pio, nor did I ask anybody else about him. The charm of the accounts I had heard on the trip between Venice and Bologne was quickly forgotten. Yet, I did find Padre Pio.

A few months after that trip, I received an invitation from some Franciscan sisters to visit their convent. This gave me a new opportunity to hear about Padre Pio. The Mother Superior asked me if I knew of him, and I answered that I had just heard of him. "You must get to know Padre Pio better," the sister told me, and she advised me to read a book about him. When we exchanged goodbyes, she gave me a little photograph of Padre Pio and his address.

I now knew Padre Pio's face, as well as where this Capuchin Father, "who bears the wounds of Jesus," could be found. In the next few days, I bought Alberto del Fante's book *Per la Storía (For the Record)*. In this book I read many extraordinary things about Padre Pio that filled me with enthusiasm. Yet even this reading, like the original acounts on the train trip, would have been forgotten with time, and with them the figure of Padre Pio would have fallen to the back of my mind had not a new call occurred that very year—a small but strange episode that stirred up within me, once and for all, the desire to become acquainted in person with Padre Pio.

Looking back on the last fifteen years, in which I went to see Padre Pio over seventy times, I feel compelled to share my experience with others. The good I have received from Padre Pio does not belong exclusively to me, for as I see it, the good we receive is not exclusively for us, but we receive it so that we may also give it to others.

Padre Pio's life, which was so full of sacrifices, acts of renunciation and sufferings, is a living, natural and free wellspring of benefits for us—spiritual, bodily and material benefits, depending on our need. Padre Pio's life is also a summons—often severe, but always salutary—to examine the conduct of our life. From the beginning, San Giovanni Rotondo seemed to me a strange pulpit in which Padre Pio, in his rough and simple way, offers us his teaching, with few words and much example. This teaching is a realistic invitation to simplicity, an exhortation to face our problems with the means offered to us by the Faith—in the first place, prayer and trust in its efficacy—and it is also an insistent call to follow Jesus in His Commandments and Sacraments. To love Jesus is to live ever more in God's grace: This is what Padre Pio demanded of us when we would come to visit him at San Giovanni Rotondo. As often as we succeed in putting his teaching into practice, we cannot help but observe and marvel at its extraordinary efficacy. Thus our encounters with Padre Pio are like beneficial stages that make us more content, more fervent, more apt to confront and resolve the business of life.

STORIES
OF
PADRE PIO

"And I will give you pastors according to my own heart, and they shall feed you with knowledge and doctrine."

—Jeremias 3:15

Chapter 1

THE PILGRIMAGE TO POMPEII

In order to obtain special help in a difficult situation, I thought of making a pilgrimage to the Shrine of Our Lady of the Holy Rosary at Pompeii. A dear friend of mine had once told me that in a case which was, humanly speaking, hopeless, she wanted to try one last thing. So she went on foot from Naples to Pompeii, imploring Our Lady by this sacrifice to obtain for her the grace she had so much at heart, and which she did in fact obtain.

I therefore turned once more to this friend for advice on my planned pilgrimage, which I also wanted to make on foot. My friend told me immediately that the road was long and quite fatiguing, and that it was not advisable for me to go alone. To my surprise, my friend then offered to accompany me with as much simplicity as if it were a brief walk. We chose the first Saturday of the month of the Rosary, October 1, 1949.

During this pilgrimage, there was a strange incident that brought me even closer to Padre Pio. We had already been on the road a couple of hours when, as we were passing through San Giovanni of Teduccio, a little boy came up from behind us.

He showed me a little prayerbook with a picture of Our Lady of Pompeii. Hastily, the little boy asked me, "Did you lose this?" and as he gave me the little book, he disappeared.

This little book was the *Novena of Thanksgiving to Our Lady of Pompeii*, which I had brought with me with the intention of reciting it at the end of the pilgrimage. I had put it in a tiny leather purse, which I had stuck in the pocket of my jacket. Along with the novena was the money for our return trip—3,000 lire in all—and a money order for 16,000 lire, plus a photograph of my husband, the photograph of Padre Pio from the Franciscan sisters and a little picture of the Child Jesus from Del Fante's book, with these words written on it: "Blessed by the stigmatized hands of Padre Pio."

I searched my pocket to see if the little purse was there; I found it in its place, but it was open. The photographs, the picture and the money order were missing, while the 3,000 lire for our return trip was still there. My companion advised me to turn back, at least to locate the little boy who had found and returned the novena booklet. We quickly realized, however, that, thanks to the crowded street, it was impossible to look either for the little boy or the lost objects, and so we continued on our way. Then, for the first time, my thoughts turned to Padre Pio and I addressed a prayer to him. I said several times in my heart, "Padre Pio, let me find the lost objects at home!" I even thought for a moment that I might have forgotten them at home and that I would find them when I returned. Of course, if I had lost them on the road, it was absurd to hope that anybody would return them to me at home. For although these little items were dear to me, they would be insignificant to anybody else, so whoever would have found them would have thrown them out or destroyed them. And even if somebody actually wanted to return them to me, it would not have been possible, since my name and address were not written on them anywhere. So there was no point in giving them any more thought.

So we went our way, reciting the Rosary. From time to time, though, I thought about how strange it was that I had recovered the novena of thanksgiving which I was supposed to recite at the end of the pilgrimage and that the money for our return trip home had not been lost. I could not help seeing in that a loving sign of Providence.

After a seven-hour walk, we arrived at Pompeii in the early afternoon. We were still fasting, and we received Holy Communion at Our Lady's altar. Once the prayers were over, we concluded our pilgrimage with our hearts thankful and full of faith.

During our return trip, we spoke again about the lost items, but without giving much importance to them. Nevertheless, almost as soon as I got home, I looked for them everywhere, but did not find them.

On Monday morning, October 3, the Feast of St. Thérèse of the Child Jesus, I remembered having read that Padre Pio was particularly devoted to this Saint. I thought of the lost items and said within myself, "O Padre Pio, you could have made me find them at home!" Then it occurred to me that the only thing I could still do was to go back to the place where I had gotten the 16,000-lire money order. I decided to go there the next morning, but while I was getting ready to walk out, I heard a knock on the door. I opened the door and saw the caretaker of my house with three women and a little boy, who wanted to talk to me.

Before I had time to ask them what they wanted, one of the women brusquely showed me a photograph, asking me in her southern dialect, "Do you know this man?" Did I know him! It was the photograph of my husband that I had lost on the way to Pompeii! I asked the women to come in and tell me everything, and I recognized the little boy as the same one who had returned my lost novena booklet.

"How did you find me?" I asked the women.

"The monk! This one here!" one of them answered spiritedly, laying the photograph of Padre Pio on the table. Then, still struck by the extraordinary event that had happened to her, she told me how it had come about.

Around noon on Saturday her son Michael, who had been playing in the street all morning, came back home. He had built a little altar on a table, putting the picture of the Child Jesus in the middle and the two photographs on the sides; he then decorated the little altar with flowers and two candles. Wanting to light the candles, he went to his mother, who was near the oven cooking, and asked her for "a little fire," holding out a small rolled-up piece of paper. As the woman took the piece of paper to put it next to the flame from the oven, she saw some numbers written on it; she thought it was a check from a bank and she wanted to keep it. Since she could neither read nor write, she walked over to her neighbor to ask what the paper was. But her neighbor said, "They'll say you stole it: it's a money order and it's worth 16,000 lire. Throw it in the fire; otherwise you could have trouble!"

The woman returned home somewhat disturbed but could not bring herself to burn the piece of paper; something was holding her back. That evening she went to the police station to show the piece of paper to the sergeant. The sergeant examined it and advised her to tear it up in order to avoid any problems. The woman then brought the paper home, but she could not tear it up; something seemed to be preventing her. Thus her Sunday had passed.

On Monday night she could not get any sleep; from time to time she seemed to see that monk in the photograph, who kept repeating to her, "Go to the house! Go to the house! Go to the house!" She wondered what house she needed to go to and became annoyed at the monk, who would not leave her in peace. Finally, at five o'clock in the morning, she got up and knocked on her neighbor's door again to ask her if there were an address written on the paper. When she found out the address of the company in Naples that had issued the money order, she immediately decided to go there. In order not to be alone, she took her son Michael with her and asked two friends from work—who, like herself, were laundresses—to accompany her.

They were not familiar with Naples, so it was difficult for them to find that place of business; nevertheless, they did find it. They arrived just as it was opening and found out my address. Then there was one final little mishap: The girl who had filled out my order had gotten my name wrong; and thus when the women finally reached my house, they gave the wrong name to the caretaker and were sent away. They were a little discouraged and did not know what to do; then Michael's mother thought of showing the photograph of my husband to the caretaker, who then led them to me.

"And here we are, *at the house!* Just like this monk wanted!" Michael's mother said with satisfaction. "And here are all your things! Is anything missing?"

"No," I answered, touched. "Not a thing!"

After the women had gone home, it seemed to me almost incredible that the little things I had lost on the distant road to Pompeii had been returned to me at home. The prayer that, humanly speaking, had seemed absurd, was heard to the letter! I understood then as never before that the ways of grace have a path all their own: they move along on God's own roads, which know neither obstacles nor impediments, to reach us in a prodigious manner. I understood also that it does not matter what we ask, so long as we ask for it with great simplicity.

This experience of faith, which seemed to me like an initial lesson in the school of Padre Pio, was a gift from the Pompeii pilgrimage. It was not the only gift from this pilgrimage, but it was the most surprising and unexpected one. In that same month of the Rosary, the prayer for which I had undertaken the pilgrimage was also heard; and for myself and my companion, benefits and graces accrued for some time, like one prolonged blossoming of our sacrifice. Finally, this was the pilgrimage that brought me, once and for all, to Padre Pio.

Chapter 2

THE GENERAL CONFESSION

In the Holy Year of 1950, I planned to make a General Confession and thought I might be able to do so to Padre Pio.

My devotion to Padre Pio began with the episode described in the last chapter. I often recited the novena to Our Lady of the Rosary of Pompeii for him, hoping that one day I might be able to meet him in person and that he might prepare me for a General Confession. The occasion for the General Confession was the Holy Year and my entrance into the Third Order of St. Dominic.

At that time I was not familiar with San Giovanni Rotondo, nor was I aware that Padre Pio had only a few minutes available for each Confession, which would not be enough time to make a General Confession to him. But although I was not able to make my General Confession to Padre Pio, the prayers I had said for this Confession were heard in a really extraordinary way.

What led me to make my General Confession was a new book about Padre Pio, published in March of 1950. In this book—*Padre Pio*, by Piera Delfino Sessa—I read that Padre Pio often had his penitents recite the following prayer:

> My past, O Lord, to Thy Mercy,
> My present to Thy Love,
> My future to Thy Providence!

It seemed as if this simple prayer possessed a magical force, a force I had never before experienced. These words of Padre Pio took possession of me and no longer allowed me to think of anything but my General Confession. I would have liked to leave the next day for San Giovanni Rotondo, but this was not possible. Nevertheless, I desired to make a General Confession and did not want to put it off, so I began preparing myself.

In this preparation it seemed as if somebody were guiding me step by step, and I could not help but think of Padre Pio. Thus, at the same moment that I understood I had to give up the idea of going to San Giovanni Rotondo, an inspiration came to me to make my Confession at the Shrine of Pompeii. I did not really know any priest from that shrine, but one soon came to mind: the priest who had given me Holy Communion at the end of my pilgrimage last October 1. He was an old priest, with a face full of peace and goodness. I remembered his facial features well, and although I did not know his name or whether he was affiliated with the shrine, I hoped to find him.

In that day of my preparation, I was given to understand as never before, with singular clarity, the great importance that a General Confession has for our life. It is, at the same time, an end and a beginning: the necessary and salutary end of the things of the past, and a marvelous beginning of a better future.

The next morning—Tuesday of Passion Week, March 21, 1950—I went to Pompeii. The Shrine of Pompeii was full of priests that day; perhaps there was a pilgrimage or a special convention of religious. I looked everywhere, trying to locate the priest to whom I wanted to make my Confession, but I could not find him. So I went into the sacristy, where there was only one old sacristan. I described the priest I was looking for and asked the sacristan if he knew him.

"Yes," he answered immediately. "It's Monsignor Giliberti."

"Would you do me the courtesy of calling him?" I asked. "I'd like to go to Confession to him."

The sacristan looked at me a bit perplexed and said to me sullenly, "What do you think, that he'll come down for you?"

I did not understand his answer right away, and I asked him again to call Msgr. Giliberti. But the sacristan, even more dryly, answered me, "For months, Msgr. Giliberti has no longer been coming down to the church; what then do you want? He has a very serious heart ailment; we can't call him."

I went back to the church a bit disappointed; I did not know what to do. I remembered, however, that I had brought a book specifically to give to this confessor—the book in which I had read the prayer of Padre Pio that had prompted me to stop delaying my General Confession. I went again to the sacristy to have this book sent to Msgr. Giliberti.

The sacristan was not there, but there was another priest to whom I turned. I asked him if he knew a priest whose appearance I described, and he too answered me without hesitation: "That's Msgr. Giliberti." I told the priest a little bit about why I had come to Pompeii, in the hope of making my Confession to Msgr. Giliberti.

"The Confession, unfortunately, is impossible," the priest told me kindly, "because Msgr. Giliberti has a very serious heart ailment and for some time he hasn't been able to leave his room."

"Father, could you at least bring this book to Msgr. Giliberti?"

"Gladly!" the priest answered. He took the book and told me to wait in the sacristy.

After about a half an hour, the priest returned and said to me, "Msgr. Giliberti asks you to wait near his confessional, the second one on the left."

Seeing my surprise, the priest added happily, "Yes, yes, Msgr. Giliberti wants to come down to the church. Wait for him!"

After an hour had gone by, a Redemptorist Father asked me for whom I was waiting. I answered that I was waiting for Msgr. Giliberti.

"He won't come to the church," the Father said, "and much less for a Confession—he's too sick!"

I answered that Msgr. Giliberti himself had
informed me that I was to wait for him.

"You'll wait in vain!" the priest said. Then he
asked me brusquely, "But Madam, do you have
faith?"

"Yes, Father!" I answered.

"In that case you can go to Confession to any
other priest; don't you see how many confession-
als there are here?"

It seemed to me that the priest was right, so I
said, "Father, if you think so, I could also go to
Confession to you!"

At that moment, however, somebody called this
priest, and he went away without speaking another
word to me.

Meanwhile, the bells were ringing the noon
Angelus. Rays of sunlight were penetrating through
the high stained-glass windows into the mystical
darkness of the great Basilica of the Rosary. The
entire dome, with its beautiful image of St. Dominic,
was full of sunlight. It seemed to me like an invitation, a confirmation! While I was thinking of this,
I saw the priest for whom I was waiting. I recognized him right away and went over to meet him.

"Father, may I go to Confession to you?" I asked
him.

"Certainly!"

"But would it be too much for you if I ask to
make a General Confession?"

"No, it would not be too much, my daughter!"
he answered with great kindness.

Attentively and patiently, then, he heard my Confession, which he brought to perfection down to the smallest details, so that I really could not have made a better General Confession.

After the Confession, Msgr. Giliberti said to me, "You have received a great grace, for which you must thank God and also Padre Pio!"

That day was important not only for me, but for my confessor as well. A month later, when I returned to Pompeii in April, I found to my surprise Msgr. Giliberti in his confessional. I went right over to greet him. With great joy he told me that, on the day I had gone to Confession, his health was restored and after that day he was able to resume all his priestly duties. I attributed both the grace of my general Confession and that of his health to Padre Pio's prayers and sacrifices. For that reason Msgr. Giliberti thought I should go to San Giovanni Rotondo to meet Padre Pio in person and thank him in Msgr. Giliberti's name.

At that time, a trip to San Giovanni Rotondo was impossible for me. I explained the reasons to Msgr. Giliberti, but he still thought I needed to meet Padre Pio in person. He advised me to pray that I would be able to go to see Padre Pio. That is what I did.

Before long, at the end of the same month of April, my prayer was heard in an unexpected way. I had not mentioned Padre Pio to my family, nor had I expressed to anybody my desire to go and see Padre Pio. However, one day my husband, who is a surgeon, told me that a strange thing had happened to him: all his patients at the clinic of the Brothers of St. John of God at Benevento had had a photograph of a monk. I immediately knew that this monk could be none other than Padre Pio, and I was happy with this coincidence, which had stirred up in my husband the desire to go to San Giovanni Rotondo to meet Padre Pio. Thus, my desire and that of Msgr. Giliberti was granted.

On May 1, 1950, we went to San Giovanni Rotondo, and the next morning we assisted at the Holy Mass that Padre Pio celebrated in the little old church at the altar of St. Francis of Assisi. I was profoundly struck by the person of Padre Pio, who was utterly absorbed in Christ and in Christ Crucified in the Holy Sacrifice of the Mass. I was also struck by his humility and great simplicity.

This brief but wonderful visit to Padre Pio was followed by many others. There were visits in difficult times or for "desperate" cases, when I had to ask him for advice or the assistance of his prayers, and there were visits in happy times, to thank him for graces obtained. But above all, these visits were encounters with Padre Pio, on which he put his unmistakable mark, making them extremely useful, not only for myself but for many others.

Chapter 3

A BRIEF BIOGRAPHICAL SKETCH

Padre Pio was born on May 25, 1887, at Pietrelcina, a little village in the province of Benevento.
As soon as he was born, his humble parents—Orazio
Forgione, an agricultural worker, and Maria
Giuseppa De Nunzio—put him under the protection of St. Francis, giving him in holy Baptism the
name of the Poverello of Assisi.

Francesco began his first studies in the village
where he was born, with his mother earnestly
supervising them. At the age of fifteen, in January
of 1902, he entered the novitiate of the Capuchins
in the nearby Monastery of Morcone in the
province of Benevento.

In the novitiate, Francesco distinguished himself, especially by his spirit of mortification and sacrifice. But it seemed as if his health was destined
to suffer from the many mortifications he imposed
upon himself. In fact, when his parents went to
visit him toward the end of his novitiate year, they
found him so run down and thin that in spite of
their happiness and pride in his vocation, they considered pulling him out of the monastery. Zi Orazio,
as Padre Pio's father was called, quite readily

described this episode from his son's life. He described this visit in his frank and simple manner:

"We found him so run down that we wanted to take him back home with us. However, the Father Guardian told us that, without the Father Provincial's permission, it would not be possible. And thus poor Francesco remained in the monastery."

Yes, Francesco stayed in the monastery. Who could have taken him away from it? Who could ever have induced him to return to the world? Nobody! Not even the parents he loved so tenderly. From now on he belonged to another family—the family of St. Francis of Assisi, the family of his vocation. On January 22, 1903, he donned the Capuchin habit in the Monastery of Morcone, receiving the name of Pio.

Seven years later, on the Feast of St. Lawrence, August 10, 1910, Brother Pio was ordained a priest in the Cathedral of Benevento. Only his mother Giuseppa was present at the beautiful ceremony of priestly ordination; his father had left long ago for North America as an agricultural worker, in order to allow his son to study and become a priest.

On that happy morning of August 10, 1910, Mamma Giuseppa went early in the morning on foot from Pietrelcina to Benevento. She was accompanied by her son, who, for reasons of health, was staying in his native village. After the ordination, on the same day, the young priest and his mother got back on the road like two pilgrims, returning on foot to their village almost eight miles away. Everything was just that humble and simple in Padre Pio's life!

The next day, in the parish church of Saint Mary of the Angels in Pietrelcina, Padre Pio celebrated his first Holy Mass, and Mamma Giuseppa had the joy of receiving Holy Communion from his hands. The following Sunday, August 14, in the same church, Padre Pio celebrated a Solemn High Mass for the first time.

In the next few years—until 1915, to be exact—Padre Pio had to return several times to the area of his birth for reasons of health. There he spent his days in a little straw hut he had built amidst the silence and solitude of the country, in order to better dedicate himself to study and prayer. It was there, far from the world and near to God, that Padre Pio received the invisible stigmata on September 20, 1915. In Alberto Del Fante's book, we read that on that day Padre Pio had been absorbed in meditating on the "Canticle of Brother Sun," that wonderful hymn of St. Francis of Assisi:

"O most high, almighty and good Lord, Thine be praises, glory, honor and every benediction..."

It is possible that it happened thus. But we can know little or nothing about the intimate secret of this event, which put an indelible mark on Padre Pio's entire life.

Toward the end of the same year, a new page opened in Padre Pio's religious life. On the vigil of the Feast of St. Lucy, December 12, 1915, Padre

Pio left Pietrelcina for good. It was not easy to say goodbye to his mother, his father, family members and beloved village, which he was never to see again.

Padre Pio was assigned by his superiors to the Monastery of St. Anne at Foggia, but he did not stay there long; the climate was not conducive to his health. So his superiors decided to transfer him to the Monastery at San Giovanni Rotondo, which, at an altitude of roughly 700 meters above the Gargano mountains, might be better for his health.

The question of his health was certainly the most important but not the only reason for this transfer and for the choice of a monastery as distant from the world as the Monastery of Our Lady of Grace at San Giovanni Rotondo. Padre Pio's personality already had something exceptional about it that exercised a very special charm and attraction on others—too special for a pure and simple acceptance by his superiors. The faithful flocked to the monastery of the Capuchin Fathers almost exclusively to see Padre Pio, attributing to him wonderworking powers. His superiors, who did not all agree on whether or not his exceptional character came from God, wanted to put an end to this coming and going by the faithful, and the choice of an obscure little monastery in the harsh, inhospitable Gargano region seemed to resolve the Padre Pio question for good.

"If they are roses, they'll bloom" is a common saying among prudent people when they are not

sure whether or not some extraordinary phenome-
non comes from God or from His enemy. The idea,
then, was that if Padre Pio's exceptional character
were truly willed by God, it would bear fruit even
in the most hidden place in the world; but if, on
the other hand, it came from the evil one, then
the little monastery, which was unknown and hidden in an area not easily accessible, would certainly
be the most fitting place for this case. Considered
in this light, the Monastery at San Giovanni
Rotondo was in every respect the right monastery
for Padre Pio. In fact, as time has shown, it was
the monastery that Divine Providence had chosen
for him so that his priestly mission might produce
rich blossoms and yield its finest fruits.

From 1916, Padre Pio lived in this monastery,
which was dedicated to Our Lady. There he
received the visible stigmata on Friday, September
20, 1918; there he spent the entirety of his long
and fruitful life as a religious and a priest; and there
he celebrated the fiftieth and sixtieth anniversaries
of his religious life in the Capuchin Order on January 22, 1953, and January 22, 1963, as well as the
Golden Anniversary of his priestly ordination—
August 10, 1960.

Chapter 4

A CHRISTMAS GIFT

One evening my neighbor came over in tears, along with her daughter who was barely a year old. She held out the girl, who was three feet tall, saying to me, "Measure! Claretta has one leg shorter than the other!" She put the child on the couch, and as the tears streamed down, she told me that for a number of days she had noticed that the child was limping. When she looked for the reason, she found that the girl's left leg was more than an inch shorter than her right one.

That was the beginning of a long, painful period for this poor mother. She went from doctor to doctor, from clinic to clinic, eventually taking the child to Bologne to be examined in the famous orthopedic clinic of the university. The diagnosis: congenital dislocation of the thighbone and almost a total lack of a joint on the left thighbone. The doctors believed that the child would remain deformed for her entire life.

An extremely painful time thus began for little Claretta as well. She was given a plaster cast that had to be changed every six months at Bologne. She could not move anymore or play like other children. Her outstretched legs were confined in the thick plaster cast, which also covered her tiny body up to the chest. She looked like an unfurled little butterfly with a sad little face.

Every day little Claretta could be seen on the balcony, sitting on her little wheelchair, looking at the children who were running and playing in the street down below.

In December of 1951, in the same clinic of Bologne, the cast was put on Claretta for the third time; she was supposed to keep it on for another six months. Unfortunately, in spite of the most meticulous care at home and the finest treatment in the orthopedic clinic, there was no sign of improvement, and accordingly, Claretta's parents grew increasingly discouraged.

Just then, shortly before Christmas of that same year, I received an invitation to go to San Giovanni Rotondo. As soon as my neighbor found out, she asked me to explain her great anguish to Padre Pio and request his prayers for the complete healing of her little daughter.

At the time I was not very familiar with San Giovanni Rotondo because, apart from my first brief visit on May 1 of the previous year, I had only been there one other time in passing and just to say hello very briefly; so this was my third visit. Quite readily I agreed to go for Claretta, thinking it would be easy for me to speak with Padre Pio.

From Naples to San Giovanni Rotondo is about a four-hour car ride, but having begun the trip on

Christmas Eve, I took much longer, due to a snow-storm I encountered in the Gargano mountains. San Giovanni Rotondo seemed to be buried under snow; from the mountains came an icy wind, which made the road to the monastery even harder to reach. Nevertheless, countless faithful had arrived from near and far to assist at the midnight Holy Mass that Padre Pio was to celebrate. The little Capuchin church was unbelievably crowded, and whoever had been unable to find a place in the church was stand-ing on the square before the church, oblivious to the snow and the wind.

During the midnight Mass, I was not able to get a glimpse of Padre Pio, even from a distance. At the end of this first Christmas Mass, at which Padre Pio distributed Holy Communion to hundreds of the faithful, the church was emptied of much of the crowd, but it was suddenly refilled with those who had remained outside.

I found a good place and was able to assist at Padre Pio's second Holy Mass, at which I too received Holy Communion from his hands.

At about four in the morning, Padre Pio began his third Christmas Mass. By now only a few of the faith-ful were still in the church, and I, along with a few others, took a place near the foot of the altar, where Padre Pio was celebrating. We were all extremely tired, and eventually we wound up crouching on the ground around Padre Pio the celebrant, who was the only one showing no sign of weariness.

At five in the morning, Padre Pio finished his third

Mass and accordingly left the altar. I got up and went to meet him and to wish him a merry Christmas.

It is difficult to describe Padre Pio's face, so full of humble and simple gentleness, his meek and wise glance, his voice, which can give a singular efficacy even to his simplest words.

Padre Pio went slowly towards the sacristy; suddenly he stopped and said to me with a smile, "Best wishes to you too!" This first face-to-face meeting with Padre Pio struck me profoundly, and in my emotion I forgot about Claretta!

Fortunately, however, just before he entered the sacristy, Padre Pio stopped again, and his glance reminded me of what I was supposed to ask him. The only thing I managed to say to him was, "Padre Pio, Claretta's thighbone!" Padre Pio, smiling kindly, answered, "On St. Joseph's day! On St. Joseph's day!"

When I went home and told my neighbor about this answer from Padre Pio, she did not hide her disappointment. She would have liked an immediate answer and to see the healing take place right away! From now on her suffering was great because St. Joseph's feast day [March 19] seemed too far away. Every day was a long one for her; every day that went by seemed to confirm that there was nothing more to do for her child. Thus, we did not talk any more about our attempt to get help from Padre Pio. But the child always kept with her a little photograph of Padre Pio, which I had brought from San Giovanni Rotondo.

The weeks went by, and we gave no more thought to Padre Pio's words. In any case, a new examination was not scheduled at Bologne until June of 1952, when the plaster cast was also supposed to be changed; so before that date we could not be sure of any improvement or real healing. It was logical, then, to assume that St. Joseph's feast day would go by unnoticed, without anything new.

However, St. Joseph's feast day did not go by unnoticed! On the morning of March 18, the girl's parents, to their great surprise, found little Claretta free in her bed; the plaster cast looked like it had been cut into many pieces. Frightened, and without immediately remembering Padre Pio's words, they left right away for Bologne to get a new cast. Yet the next day, *March 19, the Feast of St. Joseph*, X-rays showed that Claretta was in the process of healing. The joint on the left thighbone was well developed, which meant that Claretta would not remain deformed or lame but would be able to walk like any other healthy, normal child. The cast, then, was no longer needed; Claretta could now begin to walk. On that happy day, Claretta's parents made a promise that when the child was in a condition to walk well, all three would go to Padre Pio in thanksgiving.

On the way back to Naples, however, my neighbor did not have the courage to put the child on the ground to make her walk; the mother was afraid. After using the cast for so long, the child was still frail and her legs were too weak—or at least so her mother thought—to hold up her body; day after day, Claretta's mother put off making her walk, refusing to follow the advice of the Bologne specialists. For months she carried the child in her arms, while Claretta should have been walking. Eventually, the mother herself grew discouraged from this fear from which she could not free herself.

During Advent of 1952, I approached Padre Pio once again for Confession, during which I strongly recommended Claretta's mother to him and asked him to pray for her. Padre Pio then gave me a beautiful little picture of the Infant Jesus of Prague, telling me that Christmas time was particularly suitable for asking for graces; then, blessing the picture, he advised me to entrust everything to the Child Jesus.

My neighbor accepted the little picture from Padre Pio with great joy and followed his advice faithfully.

On Christmas Eve she went to the midnight Holy Mass, and when the procession with the Child Jesus went through the church, she asked Him for help with all her heart. Her prayers were heard right on Christmas day! In fact, as she went home, she had the great joy of seeing Claretta outside of her bed walking happily over to meet her mother! Throughout that Christmas day, Claretta never tired of running through the house, happy as a little bird that has finally had the joy of learning to fly. No less happy was the mother, who got over her tribulation that day.

The only thing left now was to fulfill the promise of going to thank Padre Pio. Claretta's mother wanted to go right away, but her husband's work schedule left very little free time for traveling. They decided to postpone their trip to Padre Pio's until the coming Easter; but then there were other difficulties, and the trip had to be put off from Easter to Christmas and again from Christmas to Easter. Years went by! Eventually, all talk about this promise died down, because Claretta's father no longer wanted to hear about it.

In the spring of 1955, when another invitation to San Giovanni Rotondo reached me, my neighbor wanted to give me a little note for Padre Pio, asking him in a few lines to pray that by next Easter her husband would finally decide to fulfill the promise; she even added that she was only able to write these few lines.

I personally gave Padre Pio my neighbor's note. On Good Friday of that same year, Claretta's father, who for so long wanted to hear no more about San Giovanni Rotondo, was suddenly struck by a desire to spend the Easter holidays with his family at Padre Pio's! He wanted to make all the preparations for this trip himself, and on Holy Saturday they left for San Giovanni Rotondo.

On Easter Sunday, then, Claretta was able to thank Padre Pio in person. She was allowed to walk over to him and even into his confessional. Claretta kissed Padre Pio's hand with devotion. No words were needed. Padre Pio welcomed her with a smile, placed his hands upon her head and blessed her. Claretta bent down and kissed Padre Pio's hand again. Then she returned happily to her parents, who were waiting for her before the confessional, profoundly moved at the simplicity of this thank-you. They clasped the girl in their arms and wept for joy.

A few years went by and the child became a young woman, a dear and good girl, the joy of her parents and all who knew her. Her mother conse-crated her to the Child Jesus, whose image Padre Pio had once given her as a Christmas present.

Chapter 5

FIRST CONFESSION TO PADRE PIO

My fourth visit to Padre Pio was in January of 1952; during this visit I went to Confession for the first time to Padre Pio.

This time it was family business that brought me to San Giovanni Rotondo. The matter at hand was a business contract that from the beginning showed signs of being unfavorable for us. Imprudently, this contract was drawn up and signed for a duration of twenty-five years. This disturbed me very much because it bound my family and me to some dishonest people for many years.

I decided to go to San Giovanni Rotondo, therefore, to ask Padre Pio in Confession for advice and the assistance of his prayers. I prepared for this first Confession to Padre Pio with a novena in honor of the Immaculate Virgin.

On Monday, January 21, 1952, it was my turn for Confession. However, at the time I was to make my Confession, I was not aware of Padre Pio's manner of concentrating entirely on essentials in the brief time available; I was somewhat embarrassed and could not say a thing. However, Padre Pio helped me, directing the Confession himself.

After he gave me absolution, he asked me, "Do you want anything else?"

"Yes, Padre Pio, the contract!" I answered immediately.

Padre Pio, however, was silent; I thought he had not heard me. After a moment he asked me again, "You don't want anything else?"

"Padre Pio, that contract . . ."

Padre Pio did not answer me; it seemed to me as if he had suddenly become deaf and dumb. When, however, he repeated his question for the third time, I suddenly knew what I had to ask him. Without hesitation I said, "Padre Pio, accept me as your spiritual daughter and be a true father to me!"

Padre Pio answered this request of mine with great affability: "I accept you, my daughter!" And he gave me his blessing.

It really was a strange Confession, completely different from what I had imagined. I had made this trip to San Giovanni Rotondo solely to receive help and advice from Padre Pio in the difficult question of that harmful contract, and on that question Padre Pio had given me no answer. I had asked him to accept me as his spiritual daughter, which I had not intended to do since I was not well versed in such things, and Padre Pio had heard this involuntary request of mine. Yet I was disappointed, very disappointed!

To make this Confession, I had had to face quite a few sacrifices, and now it looked to me as if it were in all vain; I had to go home without having settled anything, without a single word of advice from Padre Pio.

Before leaving the church, I still had to recite the prayers Padre Pio had given me for my penance: they were precisely the same prayers in honor of the Immaculate Virgin that I had used to prepare for this Confession. That seemed a bit strange to me because I had not said a thing to Padre Pio about my preparation. I asked a friend of mine, who had gone to Confession to Padre Pio before me, what prayers Padre Pio had given her as a penance. "The prayers in honor of St. Michael," she answered, adding that she had recommended herself to St. Michael for this Confession. Another friend, who had prepared herself for Confession with the novena to Our Lady of Pompeii, had had to recite the same novena as her penance.

"How could Padre Pio have known that?" my friend asked, brusquely. "That's what makes him extraordinary!" she added with enthusiasm. However, I did not feel like dwelling on this unusual fact because I was too disappointed . . .

I said my penance at the altar of the Immaculate Virgin, which was just beside Padre Pio's confessional; after that, I thought about going away. At that moment, however, a great ray of sunshine illuminated for a few instants the wall facing the top of the choir loft, so that I could easily see a painting entitled "Saint Conrad of Parzham." The ray of sunlight returned two more times, shedding its light on the image of a Capuchin brother who used to distribute bread to the poor before a convent door. It was the image of St. Conrad of Parzham, the humble Capuchin brother with whom I was not familiar. Once more I looked at the wall, which was now in darkness, so that neither the painting nor the inscription could be distinguished.

Although at the time I could not see any significance in the three rays of sunlight pointing out to me a name, a place and a Saint I was not familiar with, I did feel comforted with a new hope.

About a month later, in a church at Naples, I saw a Capuchin Father whom I had asked one day for a book about the life of a Franciscan. He had not been able to find that book, so he gave me another one, chosen by chance: it was the *Life of St. Conrad of Parzham*! With great interest I read this book, in which I also found some information about the Shrine of Altötting, the great Marian shrine in Southern Germany. This was where the Saint, whose image I had seen for the first time at San Giovanni Rotondo on the day of my first Confession to Padre Pio, spent almost his entire life.

This book seemed to me like an invitation to make a pilgrimage to that shrine, so I intended to take advantage of an upcoming trip to Germany to go to Altötting.

I had an opportunity to make this pilgrimage sooner than I had thought; I was at Altötting in May of that same year. I went first to the Church of St. Conrad of Parzham, where his relics were, and I prayed to the Saint, entrusting to him all the matters that had been close to my heart for so long. Immediately afterwards, I went to make a visit in the Holy Chapel of Our Lady. There I saw a woman carrying a large cross on her shoulders, making the rounds about the Holy Chapel on her knees. I also saw other people, either on their knees or on their feet, carrying great crosses around Our Lady's chapel. Since I had never seen anything like this, I wanted to ask in the sacristy what this pious practice meant. The sacristan explained:

"In the most desperate cases, when people can find no other solution, they promise Our Lady to carry the cross around her chapel if she will hear them."

As the sacristan told me that, he gave me a little booklet entitled *The History of the Cross of Stocker*. That same evening I read the moving story of a man named Stocker, who found himself in very grave danger from which, humanly speaking, there was no possibility of deliverance. He turned with complete trust to Our Lady, promising her to carry a heavy cross from his village to the Holy Chapel of Altötting if he were delivered from his misfortune. No sooner had he made this promise than he was heard in a truly miraculous manner. That was the origin of this devotion of carrying the cross around the Holy Chapel of Our Lady of Altötting, a devotion which has been proved extremely efficacious in the most difficult and desperate cases and has yielded, and still yields, countless graces and favors.

The next morning, as I was hearing Holy Mass in the Holy Chapel, it seemed to me that the moment had come when I too should make my promise to Our Lady. With complete faith I asked her to deliver me and my relatives from that contract, and I promised to carry the cross in thanksgiving around her chapel once for every year deducted from the twenty-five stipulated in the contract. And, although I knew that there was no way the contract could be broken so quickly, I dared to add, "But if the contract is cancelled this year, then I shall carry the cross around your chapel twenty-five times."

As I said that, I felt that Our Lady had accepted my promise, and with this certainty I left Altötting and began the journey home.

My prayer was heard that same year! The contract, which was supposed to last twenty-five years, was cancelled in less than two months. That year I also had an opportunity to return to Altötting, and in the month of October, I fulfilled my promise of thanksgiving.

So my fourth visit to San Giovanni Rotondo and my first Confession to Padre Pio were not in vain. *Nothing was in vain!*—neither the prayers, nor the sacrifices nor the bitter experiences. Everything bore fruit and gave me much more than I had hoped or asked for.

Every year in my travels it is important to me to return to Altötting for a brief pilgrimage. Every year brings its pains and joys, and there is always much to ask for and for which to give thanks. That is why, whenever I am at Altötting, I quite gladly carry the cross around the Holy Chapel of Our Lady: I carry it for myself and for my dear ones; and when I recall that I found Altötting, like so many other good things, at San Giovanni Rotondo, I carry it also each time for Padre Pio.

Chapter 6

A MARRIAGE CRISIS

In January of 1953, I was entrusted with the task of collecting offerings for the Capuchin church to be built at Padre Pio's birthplace, at Pietrelcina. It was for this collection that one evening I visited a family living in my building. I only knew this family by sight, and thus I did not know what a sad situation they were in. The family—a young husband and wife with a little daughter barely two years old—was about to split up. A marriage crisis, caused by the husband's unfaithfulness, had brought ruin to their family life. The husband, a well-to-do industrialist, had renewed relations with women he had known before his marriage, and thus discord and disorder had entered his life. Before long, everything was destroyed by this disorder: his love for his wife and little daughter, domestic peace, the joy of family life. Finally carried away by his distractions, he wanted to free himself from his family so that he could live as he pleased, undisturbed. So one day he decided to send his wife back to her parents, who were living in America.

That evening, when I went to find this family, everything was quite sad. The wife, in tears, told me about her pain. In a few days she was supposed to leave for America with her child. Her husband had arranged it thus, and everything was already prepared for the departure. Nothing more could be done; neither her tears nor her attempts at reasoning could prevent the imminent separation.

I gave the woman two medals blessed by Padre Pio.

"Yes," she told me, "Padre Pio could still save us."

She asked me to talk to her husband and suggest that he go with her to see Padre Pio before she left.

While we were speaking, her husband came in. He barely said hello, but when he found out about the collection, without hesitating he gave me a generous offering for Padre Pio's church. So I also gave him a medal and a little photograph of Padre Pio, which he accepted, immediately putting them in his pocket. That encouraged me to ask him whether or not he wanted to accompany his wife, before she left, on a brief visit to Padre Pio.

"To Padre Pio? But why?" he asked me, irritated.

I did not answer him. But he, as if moved by an inner rebellion, continued:

"To Padre Pio! What do I have to do with Padre Pio? What do we have to do, my wife and I, with this Padre Pio?"

"Padre Pio could give you some advice, help . . ."

"I don't need advice or help; I don't need Padre

Pio! I'm a young man, I'm barely twenty-eight years old . . . I want to live, Madam!"

"To live?" I asked him, a little surprised. "What do you mean by that?" He did not answer me, however.

"Do you not have everything? You have a young wife, a dear little daughter, a beautiful house, a secure future, well-being and health. Do you not have everything you need to live happily?"

He could not give me an answer.

Two days later, Mrs. R. left for America together with her little daughter, and Mr. R. began to "live" as he had anticipated and desired. From that moment on, he could go back home, undisturbed, at any hour of the night or the early morning hours; nobody any longer asked him where he was coming from. Nobody any longer disturbed him in his well-being, in this disorder he called "liberty." Now there was nobody left who by his presence or words could disturb his conscience. Now he could "live"!

On Saturday, March 21, 1953, as I was coming back from morning Mass, I saw Mr. R., who came up to me, visibly disturbed, and said, "Madam, now I am ready to go see Padre Pio. Could you come with me?"

A bit perplexed, I asked him why he wanted to go see Padre Pio now. He told me that as he was going home at a late hour, he seemed to see Padre Pio before him. It was only for a brief moment, but it had made such an impression that he could no longer think of anything but Padre Pio, and he wanted to go see him as soon as possible!

At my home, we had already decided a few days earlier that we would spend Sunday, March 22, which that year was Passion Sunday, at San Giovanni Rotondo. I could then be of assistance to Mr. R. for his meeting with Padre Pio. I gave him all the information he needed for the trip and a letter of introduction for Padre Pio; he actually wanted to leave right away for San Giovanni Rotondo, but we did not leave until the early afternoon.

By Sunday, at five in the morning, we were all at Padre Pio's Mass. Although there were many of the faithful who wanted to speak with Padre Pio, Mr. R. had a talk with the Padre just after Holy Mass, in which he asked only for the return of his wife.

"You must change your life," Padre Pio answered in a severe tone.

"I am well disposed, Padre Pio," Mr. R. said, "but I ask for your help!"

He then made his Confession to Padre Pio.

* * *

Rarely do the faces of men seem so happy and content as after they have been to Confession to Padre Pio. At Lourdes, those who have bathed in the pools of the holy grotto can easily be recognized because their faces reflect a singular happiness. At San Giovanni Rotondo, a similar

expression can be seen on the faces of those who
have gone to Confession to Padre Pio. After Confession, the men come out of the sacristy with radiant faces, they kneel near the altar, pray devoutly
and assist at the next Holy Masses. They no longer
want to be disturbed from their recollection; they
remain immovable as they meditate on Padre Pio's
words—those simple words of admonition, advice
and encouragement which Padre Pio knew how to
pour into souls.

That is what happened to our Mr. R. as well.
He came out of the sacristy radiant and immediately began praying on his knees near the high altar.
He stayed to hear all the afternoon Masses. As I
observed him now, so recollected in prayer, so fervent and serene, I thought what a change must
have occurred in his soul; I well remembered that
evening in January when he had completely
rebuffed the invitation to go and see Padre Pio. I
remembered as well his angry words at that time:
"What do I have to do with Padre Pio? I don't
need this Padre Pio! I want to live, Madam!" How
distant now were these words, and how far away
was that evening!

We left San Giovanni Rotondo in the early afternoon hours. We chose the road to Manfredonia,
instead of the shorter one through Foggia, in order
to visit the Shrine of St. Michael at Monte
Sant'Angelo. This visit was proposed by Mr. R.,
perhaps at the instigation of Padre Pio, who quite
often recommended to his penitents a visit to the

Shrine of St. Michael. With this pilgrimage we concluded Passion Sunday, which had been rich in blessings for us all.

The next day, Mr. R. telegraphed his wife in America, asking her to return as quickly as possible; he hoped it would be feasible as soon as the coming Easter. However, his wife had become sick and could not return right away.

It was not easy for her to understand the change in her husband's attitude towards herself and the haste with which he desired her to return. A period of waiting then came in which many letters were exchanged between husband and wife, during which Mr. R. went to Padre Pio many times to receive advice and assistance, which as he now said, he very much needed!

In the autumn Mrs. R. returned with her little daughter, and thus a new life began for the reunited family, which wiped out once and for all every memory of the bitter experience of the past.

Chapter 7

VISITS WITHOUT A PARTICULAR REQUEST TO MAKE

For the most part, our visits to San Giovanni Rotondo were made for some particular reason. An urgent need, the grave illness of a loved one, a family difficulty, all sorts of tribulations, great decisions to make—these were our usual reasons for going to Padre Pio.

Then came visits of thanksgiving, which we had promised to make during a difficult moment or which we felt obliged to make even without having promised it. However, the visits of thanksgiving often left something to be desired: in difficult moments people were quick to come to Padre Pio to ask for prayers and advice, but once they obtained what was important to them, they took their time making a visit of thanksgiving. Such visits were put off, at times for years! People often need God's help, as they say, to be moved to give thanks; for people never really change: just as two thousand years ago, out of the ten lepers healed by Jesus, only one knew enough to give thanks.

Few, very few were the visits without a particular request, visits for which we had no intention of asking for anything, simple visits with no ulterior motive. Yet these visits almost always brought us some surprise and answers to our prayers in unexpected ways. My fourteenth visit to San Giovanni Rotondo, August 25-26, 1953, was one such case.

My friend Rosaria—in order to please one of her relatives who had come a long way to visit her—decided to make a visit along with her to Padre Pio. Since I too had a guest who would have liked to meet Padre Pio, we decided to go to San Giovanni Rotondo together. We left early in the morning of Tuesday, August 25, 1953.

We were fortunate: we had barely arrived at San Giovanni Rotondo when we had the joy of meeting Padre Pio in the corridors of the monastery. Padre Pio was affable and asked where we had come from, and he gave his blessing to each of us. Then he said goodbye with a beautiful smile. It was a good beginning.

In the afternoon we made a pilgrimage to Monte Sant'Angelo, to the Shrine of St. Michael, and on the way back we visited the cemetery of San Giovanni Rotondo, where the parents of Padre Pio lie in repose.

The next morning, at five o'clock, we assisted at Padre Pio's Holy Mass, and with that we concluded our visit.

We left immediately because our intention was to return right away to Naples so that we could be back home in time for lunch. However, an unexpected detour took us from the main road into the

mountains, right near the villa that my friend had
rented for her family's summer vacations. So we
had to change plans, and we decided to have lunch
in my friend's villa.

This villa was located in the Avelline mountains,
in the vicinity of the little vacation resort of
Carovilli, and belonged to a lawyer. Before we got
there, my friend advised us on how to behave: We
were not to say that we had come from Padre Pio;
in fact, we were supposed to avoid any subject having to do with faith and religion. For the lawyer
was a noted freethinker and an implacable enemy
of religion and would not tolerate any such discussion in his house. Further, dear Rosaria advised
us not to take any flowers from the garden in the
villa or to ask the lawyer for any, because he would
not be willing to give them away. He kept his garden jealously and had never given away a flower
from that garden to anybody. With these instructions and admonitions from Rosaria, we reached
Carovilli.

The lawyer's villa really was a little paradise,
above all a paradise of flowers! Located on a salient
rock in the midst of the mountains, but not crushed
by them, a bit apart from the village and at a higher
altitude, it seemed like a precious jewel scintillating
with flowers, a miniature paradise coming directly
from God's loving hands.

To my surprise, however, I read a little verse
right at the entrance, written on an attractive
ceramic plate, that left no doubt about the anti-

religious, atheistic sentiments of this paradise-villa's owner. There were similar ceramic tablets practically all over the house. Clearly, then, we could not say that we had just come from Padre Pio.

The lawyer was an elderly gentleman with distinctive features that gave him a stern appearance; he greeted us affably. Rosaria introduced us and asked the lawyer to join us for coffee. The lawyer gladly accepted the invitation and promised to show us his garden. We then left him and went into the part of the villa rented by Rosaria.

After lunch we all got together, including the lawyer, in the drawing room to have coffee. None of us knew what to talk about, and it was a bit awkward for us all to be there together. But when we went for a walk in the garden with the lawyer guiding us, he was so good at telling us about his flowers that I followed him with great interest. We understood each other quite well, because I too love flowers very much.

While we were talking, it struck me as quite strange that a man so fascinated by the beauties of nature could be so averse to God, the Creator of these beauties. I was taken by this consideration when the lawyer said to me, "Look, Madam, I'm already an old man; I don't have many more years to live. The thought that I must leave this garden some day is quite bitter to me." As if to wrest himself from this sudden disturbance, he added, half in jest and half seriously, "But I made a pact with the devil."

"With the devil?" I asked, surprised.

"Yes! For my whole life I have served him well enough; after my death he must compensate me by allowing me, every so often, to return to my garden, to my flowers."

"But Counselor, you don't really want to go to Hell?"

"Yes! yes! The devil is my best friend!"

"I don't believe that, Counselor! I think your best friends are rather these beautiful flowers of yours!"

And with that, our conversation was over. Rosaria had already given me a signal not to continue in this vein, and I too deemed it wiser to cut off our discourse. Considering the verses written on the ceramic plates, it seemed to me that this brief dialogue of ours was already something.

I reflected: if a man believes in the existence of the devil, Hell and life after death, it should not be so hard for him to believe also in the existence of God, Paradise and the immortality of the soul. I found just one answer to my reflection: in this man's life, *Jesus Christ* was missing, and therefore everything was upside down, confused and wrong. As soon as Jesus would enter that soul, everything would change! I thought about Padre Pio, from whom we had just come, and I wondered whether we had come here purely by chance or whether all of this had a certain purpose. I asked the Lord for a sign: if, contrary to all expectation, the lawyer would give me a flower from his garden, that would be a sign that our unintended trip from San Giovanni Rotondo to Carovilli was not in vain. I also promised to put this flower before the image of the Sacred Heart of Jesus later on.

To Rosaria's great surprise, and to my equally great joy, when we left, the lawyer gave me some beautiful roses and some other precious flowers from his garden!

At home that same evening, I put these flowers, just as I had promised, before the image of the Sacred Heart of Jesus—*for the conversion of the lawyer of Carovilli.*

After that splendid day, August 26, 1953, time passed: weeks, months, years! I occasionally asked Rosaria, to whom I had not confided my secret prayer and hope, for some news about the lawyer of Carovilli. "He's always the same! He'll never change!" was the constant reply.

During Passion Week of 1955, I prepared to go to Confession to Padre Pio. The day I left for San Giovanni Rotondo, I found out from Rosaria that the lawyer of Carovilli was very sick; I planned to recommend him to Padre Pio.

On Friday of Passion Week, April 1, 1955, I went to Confession to Padre Pio. It was also the first Friday of the month, consecrated to the Sacred Heart of Jesus; that gave me a great deal of hope that I could do something for the lawyer of Carovilli. In fact, after my Confession, it was easy for me to explain to Padre Pio about the lawyer's situation. Padre Pio promised to pray for him and urged me to write to him immediately, without any hesitation, inviting him to use the opportunity of the upcoming Easter to be reconciled with Jesus in the Holy Sacraments. Padre Pio also blessed a little picture of the Sacred Heart of Jesus and a rosary for the sick man.

That same morning, following Padre Pio's advice, I wrote the lawyer a letter and mailed it, together with the little picture of the Sacred Heart, from San Giovanni Rotondo. A few days later, from Naples, I sent the lawyer the rosary blessed by Padre Pio.

Just after Easter the following letter arrived from Carovilli:

Carovilli, April 12, 1955

My good Lady,

I well remember you and the flowers I offered you on that day so long ago. Oh! I would not have imagined then that I would receive your letter, overflowing with goodness, which led me, by its call, to receive Jesus on the occasion of Holy Easter . . .

A similar appeal was often addressed to me by my loved ones, but I must tell you that your letter, which was quite permeated with the Christian spirit, carried great weight in my decision, and on Holy Thursday a friar of St. Francis brought me Holy Communion.

Immediately afterwards, on the same morning, your package reached me, and I was quite pleased with the beautiful rosary, on which a prayer shall be said for you too.

My joy at receiving this letter was immense; with Franciscan simplicity, it brought me the news of this great conversion. It was a profound, complete conversion, which turned this once rebellious soul into a soul on fire for God, the Sacraments and prayer. For the rest of his life, the lawyer from Carovilli loved with gratitude the gift of faith that his reconciliation with Christ had brought him.

As I thought about this conversion, I could not help but think of Padre Pio as well, and his humble life of prayer and sacrifice. For the great conversion of this man—who for over sixty years had lived far away from God, from the Faith and from the Sacraments—is connected directly to Padre Pio, who has opened to many the way to Christ and often moves us too, who live in the Faith, along the paths of God's providence to make us instruments for the conversion of men.

Every conversion has its own way, its own balance, the very delicate and precise one of Divine Justice. Thanks to God's mercy, every conversion is the result of prayers and sacrifices of those who live fervently in the Faith of Christ. The fervor of the converted ones, in its turn, causes new conversions to arise; and this is the blossoming of the Cross of Christ, the holy and consoling blossoming that will know no end, but will continue in the souls of men until the end of time.

Chapter 8

THE CONFESSOR

It is said of St. Clement Maria Hofbauer that he knew how to conquer human hearts by his great simplicity and that even the simplest words spoken by him had an extraordinary efficacy.

The same thing could be said about Padre Pio. His simple words, his brief counsels, admonitions or encouragements, as well as his sober answers had an utterly exceptional efficacy: they would strike the heart profoundly and could shake up consciences in a surprising manner. This efficacy was felt above all in *Confession*.

My first Confession to Padre Pio, which I referred to earlier, was followed by many others; I prepared for each one of them with prayer. I quickly realized that prayer is of great importance in contacts with Padre Pio. If I was well prepared, the very few minutes available were plenty. At times it struck me as extraordinary how these few minutes went by during which the Confession unfolded, along with my requests and recommendations and Padre Pio's answers. There was time for everything! The utmost economy in the use of time was noticeable in Padre Pio; in everything, he concentrated on the essentials. There were no useless words or room for discussions, which for that matter would be utterly superfluous with Padre Pio. Right from the beginning, he would interrupt the conversation with a few inspired words capable of directing us towards the solution of our problems.

His language often had a rough realism that could surprise us, particularly in our first few confessions, and leave us a bit perplexed. However, once we got used to his manner, we saw that it was useful and salutary for us.

For the most part, confessions to Padre Pio began with his asking us how long it had been since our last Confession. This first question established contact between Padre Pio and the penitent; it suddenly seemed as if Padre Pio knew everything about us. If our answers were unclear or inexact, he would correct them; we would get the feeling that Padre Pio knew us, that his eye could see our soul as it really was before God.

Padre Pio as a confessor acted like a surgeon, who necessarily wounds us in order to heal. If there were any evil in us, he would get right to the bottom of it in order to take it out, root and branch. However, this rough and severe manner of his was never arbitrary and never unjust. His only intention was to cure us of our evils, and therefore our confessions to him were always salutary.

We could not seek in Padre Pio a consoler of our pains, because only rarely did he have words of compassion for us and for our tribulations. Yet his words always had the power to give us new strength and courage. In Confession, Padre Pio was above all a *dispenser of new strength* who effectively helped us to bear the vicissitudes of life. He taught us that it is unwise to let ourselves be disturbed by our troubles and exhorted us at the same time to face them with the means that faith offers us. Padre Pio tolerated neither sadness nor discouragement in us; he pushed us towards prayer as the most efficacious means of resolving our problems. He exhorted us to trust in God and in Divine Providence. His way of helping us was a strong, radical one. He often took from us the pains we had brought with us into his confessional; it was as if he absorbed them without so much as giving us a word. In other cases, and not infrequently, he strengthened us with a few inspired words, so that we might better carry a given cross. The same cross that had seemed too heavy for our strength became, with his words and his example, light and quite bearable.

Thus, in one Confession I complained that a certain family problem seemed to me unbearable. Padre Pio, however, answered me only with a brief question: "And you really can't bear this?" as if to say, is such a trifling thing really so heavy for you? With that question I recognized how petty my problem was and resolved not to take it so seriously any more; that was quite useful for me and helped me to free myself from it.

In another Confession, I told Padre Pio about a

certain injustice, which seemed like a great cross to me. I asked him how I should behave. Padre Pio answered me: "Put up with it! It will become light!" And that is exactly what happened. Then I happened to read the following saying of Padre Pio:

"Act in such a way that the sad sight of human injustice may not trouble your soul; it too has its value in the plan of things. And upon it, one day, you will see the unfailing triumph of God's justice arise!"

Later on, I was able to experience the truth of these words in my case as well. Precisely through the injustice that I had suffered, I received an unexpected benefit in a moment of particular need.

Padre Pio dealt with me very severely for a certain lukewarmness of mine, by which I sometimes neglected prayer or the fulfillment of promises made in difficult times. Padre Pio never wanted to release me from promises or vows I had made, but he pointed out to me the way to faithfully fulfill the commitments undertaken, and he also obtained for me the strength and the fervor to do so.

For years I had committed myself to do one hour of the Perpetual Rosary on the seventh day of each month. Unfortunately, I often neglected this commitment. When I used to confess this shortcoming, I was never reprimanded, although there were no excuses for me since I had both the time and the freedom to give this one hour a month. Thus, I remained in my lukewarmness. Only a Confession to Padre Pio delivered me from it. I had hardly told Padre Pio about this negligence of mine when I received an unexpected rebuke:

"Unfortunate woman!" he told me. "Don't you know that we must be alert on the road to salvation? Only the fervent succeed in reaching it, never the tepid or those who sleep!"

These words of Padre Pio remained so impressed upon me that from then on I never neglected my commitment again.

* * *

During a grave illness, an acquaintance of mine—Elisa R.—made a vow that if she were healed, she would take up a collection in honor of Jesus Crucified, for the benefit of a particularly poor and needy church. Elisa was healed in a short time and, in the initial fervor of her gratitude, she immediately wanted to devote herself to the promised collection. However, she soon ran into various difficulties; some of her acquaintances refused to give offerings, while others hardly gave a pittance. The mortification of asking for alms seemed to her too difficult and pointless, so she decided to ask Padre Pio in Confession to dispense her from her vow and let her substitute some other good work which was easier.

Padre Pio did not dispense her from the vow but exhorted her instead to pray fervently to Jesus Crucified so that she might faithfully fulfill the vow she had made. Elisa followed Padre Pio's advice, and before long she found generous donors through whom she quickly collected the sum she had promised for the poor church. Shortly after fulfilling her vow, she received yet another grace for which she had long prayed and which for some time she had despaired of receiving.

A GENTLEMAN IN MOURNING

In the lunchroom of Our Lady of Grace Hotel at San Giovanni Rotondo, I saw at a little table a gentleman dressed in black, obviously in mourning. Yet the expression on his face was radiant, as if reflecting a great inner joy. It struck me as a strange contrast. I did not have an opportunity to speak to him in the hotel, but later on we were in the same compartment on the train during the return trip.

As often happens, some travelers asked those of us who had boarded the train at Foggia whether we had been to see Padre Pio. When we said yes, they asked us to talk about him. The gentleman in mourning did not hesitate; in fact, he seemed quite happy to be able to talk about Padre Pio and his own experience. He told us the following story:

A few days ago they killed my only son, who was barely sixteen years old. I was overwhelmed with sorrow, and it seemed as if I could never again rise from my despair. Nobody could console me. However, some time ago a friend of mine told me about a certain Padre Pio, but I didn't want to hear about him then. For years I had abandoned my family—my wife, my daughter and my son—and I lived with a woman. My life was in chaos; nothing was sacred to me anymore. And then, all of a sudden, misfortune! There I was, oppressed by such despair that the memory of Padre Pio's name seemed like an anchor of salvation! I felt as though I might be able to find a bit of comfort from him— from him alone! How this thought came to me, I don't know. But I couldn't resist any longer, and I took the first train that went south from Milan. I was finally able to meet Padre Pio yesterday. I got on my knees as if to go to Confession—but without the slightest intention of making a real Confession— and I said to him: "Padre Pio, they have killed my only son!"

I said that because I wanted a word of comfort from him. But Padre Pio, looking at me sternly, had only this brief question for me:

"And that's not enough for you?"

I was struck by these words, and I understood in an instant what I had not understood for many years. My entire life with all its errors stood before me.

"Yes, Padre Pio!" I answered.

"What are you waiting for?" he asked me. I understood what he meant by that, and I asked him if he could hear my Confession.

Since then I have been the happiest man in the world, in spite of my great mourning. I had hoped to find comfort and consolation from him, but he gave me much more: he completely transformed me!

Now I'm going back to my home, to my wife, to my daughter . . . I'm going home with a serene heart!

A WOMAN FROM GENOA

One evening we were sitting around the fireplace in the living room of Our Lady of Grace Hotel. It was a good time to compare notes about our experiences at San Giovanni Rotondo. The person most anxious to describe her own experience was a distinguished lady from Genoa, who was supposed to have made her Confession to Padre Pio that morning. However, when her turn came, the only thing she could say was, "Padre Pio, four years ago I lost my husband and I haven't gone to church since then."

"Because you lost your husband, you also lost God? Go away! Go away!" Padre Pio had told her brusquely, and he quickly closed the grates of the confessional without giving her any further attention.

The woman could not believe her ears, because nobody had ever dared to speak to her that way. What could she do? All she could do was get up and go away. She had made a long trip from Genoa and had to wait several days until her turn came for Confession, and the only words Padre Pio had had for her were, "Go away!" The death of her husband had been too great a blow for her after so many years of a happy marriage, which had never been darkened by any shadow. She had thought that Padre Pio would understand her pain for the loss of her husband and give her the comfort of a good word. Instead, to her great disappointment, she had been sent away—and in such a way!

When she left Padre Pio's confessional, however, she suddenly felt a very keen desire to be reconciled with God. So she went back to one of the Capuchin Fathers and explained her situation to him. That same morning she made, in her own words, the best Confession of her life. She was very happy, and she attributed the merit of the recovery of her faith to the way Padre Pio had treated her. She then received Holy Communion from Padre Pio himself, her first one after years away from the Sacraments.

The day she left San Giovanni Rotondo, she came across Padre Pio again, and this time he gave her some words of encouragement, followed by his blessing. Thus, she too was able to go home with a content and serene heart.

"DON'T FEEL SORRY FOR YOURSELF ANYMORE"

A woman I was acquainted with, who lived at

San Giovanni Rotondo, had suffered badly from rheumatism for some time. One day, with great exertion, she dragged herself into church to go to Confession to Padre Pio. After Confession she lamented over her pains and asked Padre Pio to help her. Padre Pio gave her no answer. She was offended and said, "Ah, Padre Pio, don't you have any compassion for me? I suffer so much! Include me in your prayers!"

Before he closed the grates of the confessional, Padre Pio said to her, "Don't feel sorry for yourself any more."

A bit disappointed and also a bit offended, she left the confessional, but she had barely taken her first steps when she observed, to her amazement, that she had no more pain and could walk easily.

THE LITTLE WHITE LIE

In one Confession I told Padre Pio that I had told a lie "out of courtesy," namely, one of those lies that unfortunately are spoken too easily out of convenience when it seems more courteous and more useful to tell a lie instead of the truth.

Padre Pio immediately said to me, "What kind of courtesy can it be, if through it God is offended by a lie?"

In his inimitable way, he went on to make me understand that no courtesy or convenience could ever justify the offense given to God by a lie.

Since then I have never forgotten his brief and

rough reasoning in defense of the truth, and I have learned to be careful to no longer offend the truth for any reason.

In every Confession Padre Pio would put me in the presence of God. The image we might have of ourselves never had any importance in Confession to Padre Pio. He would take that away from us immediately, in order that we might not delude ourselves and might learn to live ever more in the reality of God's presence.

THE UNPOLISHED DIAMOND

Padre Pio's answers were not always brief. When it was necessary, he also gave more detailed responses.

My fifteenth visit to San Giovanni Rotondo, in December of 1953, had a particular reason. I had just returned from a trip abroad. During a pilgrimage, a priest had spoken to me about the so-called Caux Movement, which was fairly well known and discussed at that time. He requested that I ask Padre Pio what to think of this movement. The priest himself had been at Caux, and what he told me showed that many, including some priests, were exposed to the danger of a deception. He therefore wanted me to ask Padre Pio for prayers and advice.

On Monday, December 14, 1953, I had an opportunity to go to Confession to Padre Pio, and I explained to him about this movement, which did not want to be known as a sect but had certain principles that caused some people to call it the "antechamber of Catholicism."

Padre Pio listened to what I had to say with attention and interest. He promised to pray above all for the priests so that they would recognize the deception, for that is what it actually was. Then, pronouncing each word with that characteristic manner of his, which stamps them indelibly on our minds, he said:

"Remember: every sect in the world feeds off of the Catholic Church. Our Holy Catholic Church is like a great and extremely precious unpolished diamond, from which every so often somebody takes a particle and polishes it—not without the help of the evil one—so that it begins to shine better than the great unpolished diamond. And this shine draws men, dazzles them and deceives them, so that the particle necessarily is worn out and comes to nothing. This is the game of deception, which appears and reappears with time. Jesus warned us to watch out for it!"

A SOCIALIST FROM PALERMO

I was once making the same return trip from Foggia to Naples. In my compartment there were two women from Messina and a couple from Palermo.

"I believe," said the man from Palermo, "that we have all made the same pilgrimage."

Yes, we were all coming back from San Giovanni Rotondo after the celebration of Padre Pio's fiftieth priestly anniversary. It was August 11, 1960.

The two women from Messina told us that this was already the third time they had made the long journey from Sicily to San Giovanni Rotondo to recommend some of their family problems to Padre Pio, and that this time they had come in thanksgiving for the help they had received. I also talked about my visits to Padre Pio. But the most interesting account during this trip was offered by the gentleman from Palermo. Like all of Padre Pio's penitents, he told us with frankness and without any human respect about his life before he knew Padre Pio and the completely different life he led after meeting the Padre:

I come from a background of socialism. Not that I had political ambitions or considered politics a profession or a secure source of gain or an easy life. Socialism was for me an ideal— at least that's how I conceived it then. I was troubled by the fact that there are so many poor people who don't have anything, even bare necessities; while on the other hand, there are so many rich people who have everything, even beyond what they need. I was troubled at seeing so many injustices, which hit the poor above all. I saw in socialism the solution to the problems of the poor.

Some years ago, when I first heard of Padre Pio, I suddenly felt an attraction towards him, and I wanted to explain my political point of view to him. Yet because I knew that Padre Pio was above all a confessor and that only questions of conscience could be discussed with him in Confession, I hesitated for a long time to undertake the trip to San Giovanni Rotondo. For years Socialism had taken me away from any sort of religious practice, and so it was difficult for me to decide to make a Confession. Finally, my desire to meet Padre Pio won out. However, before I left, in order to avoid carrying with me the crushing weight of sins from many years spent away from the Church, I made a Confession at Palermo, in which I freed myself from most of the weight, but not all. For my Confession to Padre Pio, I reserved some questions of conscience and primarily my political opinion.

In my first Confession to Padre Pio, only a few words were exchanged:

"Padre Pio I'm a socialist . . . but out of pure idealism!"

"Beautiful idealism you have!" Padre Pio answered with dry irony.

I had intended to tell Padre Pio the reasons that led me to this "ideal," but suddenly I sensed that no further "reasoning" was needed: my "idealism" was false, and therefore my reasons for it were also erroneous. I understood all this while I was on my knees before Padre Pio; so I merely said, "But now, Padre Pio, I no longer think so."

The absolution that Padre Pio gave me after Confession was for me like a new light leading to a new life.

When I returned to Palermo, I had to undergo not a few struggles in order to separate myself for good from my political companions! A second Confession to Padre Pio helped me to overcome the ideological difficulties, and once again it was the absolution that made me happy and made me understand that I had overcome everything by means of the Faith.

My third Confession to Padre Pio was a bit after the political elections; by now I was completely free from my original ideas. It was clear to me that neither Socialism nor any other materialistic system would ever be able to resolve the problems of the poor and of human misery in general. I also understood that religion, which is the strength and sustenance of innumerable souls, cannot be taken from human life, nor should it be deprived of its freedom. Without religion and the freedom to practice religion, the poor themselves, and especially the very poor, would be hit the hardest and exposed to infinitely more bitter miseries.

I told Padre Pio that this time I had not voted for Socialism.

"For whom did you vote, then?" he asked me.

"For nobody," I answered, "because just as I couldn't bring myself to vote for Socialism, neither could I bring myself to vote for my old adversaries. Therefore I didn't vote for anybody."

"Then you can look for absolution elsewhere," said Padre Pio dryly, and he sent me away without giving me absolution.

I was not expecting this kind of treatment, and it caused in me a serious crisis of conscience. I felt as though I had been cast into the abyss. It took me some time to understand that Padre Pio was right. In fact, for a Catholic, politics and parties are not necessary, because he finds his doctrine in his religion, in his faith, which can order his life down to the smallest details, resolving even his social problems. A Catholic would not need to get involved in the political activism of others if this activism did not contain grave dangers for his faith and its freedom. But because parties do exist that close the churches and unscrupulously restrict one of man's most precious goods, namely, his spiritual and religious freedom, a Catholic must be vigilant in defense of his faith and freedom and must not shirk the duties that the political activity of others imposes on him.

It was not long before I desired to go to San Giovanni Rotondo again. In fact, I tried at first to resist this inner call, but it became even more insistent; eventually, I took advantage of the first available vacation to return to Padre Pio.

My fourth Confession to him was unforgettable. Padre Pio welcomed me like a true father, and from then on there was no longer any shadow between us. Whenever I can, I go to him; nobody ever goes to San Giovanni Rotondo in vain. Everything there seems to have a particular meaning and a special lesson. Take this example: the other evening we reached San Giovanni Rotondo exhausted after a tiring journey, and after looking for a long time we found lodging that could not have been more uncomfortable. My wife criticized me because I hadn't thought of reserving a room, and I got terribly angry—for that matter I tend to get angry easily. Yesterday morning, after the celebration in church, when I walked over to the monastery to give my best wishes to Padre Pio, I was struck by an inscription over one of the cells which I had never seen before although I had passed through that part of the monastery many times. I read:

"Don't lose your temper! Only fools lose their temper!"

These words seemed to have been written just for me, and I resolved to keep them in mind as a warning. You see, that's how

it is at San Giovanni Rotondo: innumerable people go there, and yet for each one
there are just the right words!

We had now reached Naples. It was the end
of my trip, while the Sicilians still had a long
journey to make. We said goodbye cordially. We
were all content, as always happens after a visit
to Padre Pio.

FOR A CONVERSION . . .

In one Confession I asked Padre Pio for advice
about the conversion of a person particularly
dear to me. A complicated chain of events stood
in the way of this conversion, like an insurmountable obstacle, so that humanly speaking
there was no longer any hope. After explaining
the case to Padre Pio, I asked him:

"Padre Pio, how must I pray and what must I
do to obtain this conversion?"

Padre Pio did not give me any formula of
prayer, nor did he talk to me about "offering up"
or "putting up with" anything: for this kind of
desperate case, he could show only one way, a
way that is more difficult than praying, offering
up or putting up with anything. He told me:

"Bear everything in peace! Put everything on
the scales of Divine Justice for this conversion!"

Since that Confession, I have tried to put into
practice this wonderful, salutary, efficacious "bear

everything in peace." It is not easy to attain, but once that point is reached, it is easy to stay there and not to abandon it. "Bear everything" means much more than "putting up with everything," for when we put up with everything, it is all still a weight: troubles, tribulations, pains and even God's will seem heavy to us, too heavy! That is why in "putting up with" things we can never find true peace, because the "putting up" is still subject to our own more or less hidden rebellion, which, like a drop of poison that ruins the best wine, robs the sacrifice of its efficacy.

In this "bear everything in peace," nothing any longer is a weight, because we move in the midst of the peace and joy of God's love, which makes everything easy, which guides and strengthens us and by which alone we want to be guided and strengthened. Nothing any longer disturbs God's action in us and through us, and thus there is no longer any obstacle to the efficacy of our efforts on behalf of others.

I once wrote to a learned German Capuchin Father about my experience in Confession with Padre Pio. The following lines are taken from his letter of response:

"What you write to me about Padre Pio's efficacious manner as a confessor agrees with what mystical theology teaches, namely, that as a soul makes progress in perfection, the gifts of the Holy Ghost become ever more evident, so that we need not be astonished at the wonderfully inspired advice and answers and their exceptional efficacy."

The response of this priest, by which I conclude this chapter on Confession to Padre Pio, can serve as an answer for those who ask how it is possible that Confession to Padre Pio, though most often consisting of only a few words and brief exchanges, can act so strongly upon souls, to the point of transforming their entire spiritual life and enriching it in an exceptional way.

Chapter 9

PRAYERS HEARD

Receiving the grace of having our prayers heard is a fact of faith that always moves us insofar as it shows us, in a very special way, the loving intervention of Divine Providence in our lives.

Each granting of a prayer has its own way, its own Saints, its own pilgrimages, its own conditions. Whenever our prayers are heard, it is a manifestation of God's mercy. Before that happens, however, the mystery lies hidden. We do not know beforehand the ways and the conditions; we do not know which Saint the mediation has been entrusted to, or which sacrifice, which prayers, which pilgrimage may lead to the grace we are seeking. How then can we receive it? Through faith, through our humble and at the same time daring attempt to draw down upon us God's mercy and providence. God has sewn a desire into our heart, and we begin to pray so that it may be heard. Often, however, we see that our own prayers are not enough; it seems that our own strength is not enough to carry our prayers to Heaven, while the desire to obtain the grace requested burns ever more in our heart. So we look for somebody who can help us, and we turn to those whom we know are more fervent than we are, who are more versed in how to pray and offer sacrifices and thus are more united to Christ and even more deeply rooted in God's grace. We have confidence in the assistance of these fervent souls who are powerful in Christ, who resemble the finest mountain guides; we can securely fasten ourselves to their ropes and thus happily reach the top. As there are always new people who receive from God all the qualities needed to be good guides on mountain paths, even so there are always new people to whom God gives all the gifts needed to be a precious source of help in our need. One of these instruments of God in our time was unquestionably Padre Pio.

His mission called innumerable souls to San Giovanni Rotondo. We had recourse to Padre Pio to ask him for advice in our difficulties; we wrote to him so that he would include our problems in his prayers, telling him about whatever was close to our hearts. Padre Pio would answer, directly or indirectly, and give counsel and assistance. His answers for the most part were extremely brief, his advice was given in a few words. The way he helped us was rooted in God's providence; he himself showed that he had no part, no merit in the mediation of graces.

Of the very many cases I recommended to Padre Pio during my visits and by letter, not one answer resembled another. For every single case he had a special piece of advice, an unexpected remedy. His answers were never arbitrary. He himself told us what God's merciful providence wanted to tell us through him, and that is why he was so effective. Padre Pio was, in the true sense of the word, an instrument of Providence for us and an expert guide on the way of faith, which leads to our prayers being heard. Out of the many examples I could give, I choose the following two cases. One of them has to do with the healing of a grave physical illness, and the other involves a healing from a long-standing spiritual suffering.

In December of 1955, a friend of mine asked me to recommend urgently to Padre Pio her husband, who was stricken with a grave paralysis. Since I had to go to San Giovanni Rotondo just about that time, I promised my friend that I would speed up my trip and recommend this case to Padre Pio.

I left on December 14, and when I arrived at San Giovanni Rotondo, I wrote these few lines to Padre Pio: "Padre Pio, pray that Mario N. may again be able to move his arms and legs, and that he may be healed and restored to his family." That was all I wrote; nothing further was necessary. With Padre Pio, everything was extremely simple and concentrated on the essentials.

The following morning I went to Padre Pio's Holy Mass, and afterwards I received permission to approach him at his confessional. I gave Padre Pio my note and asked him to bless a medal for the sick man. Padre Pio immediately took my note, blessed the medal and then said, "Tell him to go afterwards to St. Nicholas, to thank him!"

In this simple and unexpected answer, everything was included: the sick man's healing and the way that would lead to this grace. Anybody who was not familiar with Padre Pio might find the answer and the interpretation to be strange, but I was already used to his way and to his answers. I knew then that I had received a good answer and that my friend's request would be granted. However, I did not know that on the same day I would be making yet another pilgrimage to the Shrine of St. Nicholas at Bari. But by one of those coincidences that occasionally happen—and happen especially at San Giovanni Rotondo!—I suddenly had to go to Bari. That certainly had not been part of my original plan, nor did I immediately decide to go, but later on, when I remembered Padre Pio's answer, I thought that the trip to Bari might also serve for a brief visit to the Shrine of St. Nicholas for my poor suffering friend. For that reason I did not want to put off my duty, which called me so unexpectedly to the nearby city of Bari, so I left immediately.

In the little bit of free time available while I was there, I went to the Basilica of St. Nicholas and prayed over the Saint's tomb for the healing of the sick man. I also got a little bottle of the "Manna of St. Nicholas," which I brought to my friend for her husband.

The same evening that I returned from Bari, December 15, 1955, my friend and her husband promised in a vow that they would go on a pilgrimage of thanksgiving to the Shrine of St. Nicholas at Bari if the healing were obtained.

And the healing was obtained! The request contained in the few lines written to Padre Pio was granted to the letter! On September 1, 1956, my friend and her husband fulfilled their vow, going first to Bari to thank St. Nicholas and then to San Giovanni Rotondo to thank Padre Pio.

The other case had to do with a long period of psychological suffering caused by a great sorrow. An acquaintance of mine—Mrs. Renata L.—had been in mourning for ten years, owing to the death of her little daughter, her only one, who was barely six years old. Renata was inconsolable; her state of mind grew worse from year to year; her faith was shaken. During her little daughter's illness, she had gone to Holy Mass every day; she had received Holy Communion every day; she had prayed much and made many promises; but nothing had been able to keep her beloved little daughter on this earth. Maria Rosa—a beautiful child of exceptional goodness and uncommon religious sentiments—died like a little Saint shortly before her sixth birthday, leaving her parents in indescribable mourning.

Ten years had gone by since then. In this case, time had not healed the wound; on the contrary, it seemed as if her sufferings and grave psychological depression were continually increasing.

One day the woman was advised to turn to Padre Pio. In spite of her skepticism, she immediately began clinging to the idea that Padre Pio could help her. In August of 1953, when she found out that I was going to visit San Giovanni Rotondo, she asked me to give Padre Pio a letter from her and earnestly to recommend her case to him.

During my visit I had an opportunity to give this letter to Padre Pio, and although there was not enough time to give a detailed recommendation, I still received a response. When Padre Pio left the church to go into the sacristy, he said as he passed in front of me, "Tell her to do something for St. Francis!"

I immediately passed on this advice of Padre Pio to Renata. My letter was mailed from San Giovanni Rotondo and arrived right on her birthday, and thus was particularly agreeable. Renata was also pleased with Padre Pio's advice, and she intended to follow it.

She still had in her possession a very rich little dress that had belonged to her daughter Maria Rosa. Renata had never wanted to touch it for any reason and was keeping it jealously as a precious memento. But as soon as she found out about Padre Pio's advice, she began to wonder whether it might make more sense to give this dress to someone who might need it. Before long, she packed up her daughter's clothes in some suitcases and brought them to an orphanage run by the Franciscan Sisters, who were known as "Stigmatines," owing to their particular devotion to the wounds of St. Francis. Seeing in this orphanage so many poor children, orphaned and in some sense abandoned by their own parents, she had a desire to do something more for these little children, and she wanted to adopt one of them in place of Maria Rosa. However, she first wanted to know Padre Pio's opinion. So in one of my Confessions, I asked Padre Pio to give his advice on the question. In general Padre Pio was not in favor of adoption; in this case, however, he was flatly opposed to it because there were two sons in the family who were already young men. So he discouraged the adoption and proposed instead that the woman take care of one of the poorest orphan children who showed signs of a vocation to become a sister, so that this child, thanks to the woman's help, could fulfill her aspiration to religious life.

As soon as the woman found out about Padre Pio's advice, she went back to the orphanage and asked if there was a poor orphan who wanted to become a sister. She found an extremely poor girl who had a vocation to the Order of the Stigmatines of St. Francis. Renata took care of her, offering her a dowry and clothes and meeting all her needs so that the young woman could leave immediately for the novitiate at Florence.

Like a real mother, Renata followed this "daughter" step by step. And when the girl entered religion, she took the name of Maria Rosa. Renata often visited the young sister at Florence and did her best to make the feast of her investiture, and later that of her solemn profession, joyful feasts not only for Sister Maria Rosa and her community, but also for her own family.

Later on she did even more for St. Francis: she contributed generously to the collection for the church of the Capuchin Fathers which was to be built at Pietrelcina, offering the altar of St. Francis. She did all this with joy and fervor, because since the day she had brought Maria Rosa's dress to the poor orphans of St. Francis, she had been delivered, as if by a miracle, from her depression. A new life began for her in which she had also recovered the gift of faith. In fact, she had always done everything in memory of her beloved daughter, but whereas at first Maria Rosa's memory had stirred up in her only tears, mourning and bitterness, it was now an incentive to good works, which in turn made up all the joy in her life. So in this case St. Francis, the Saint of joy, who had banished sadness as an obstacle to the praise and gratitude due to God, was just the right doctor!

With a few simple but highly inspired words, Padre Pio had been able to lead her to these graces and to all the good that followed from them. That can only be explained by his mission from God, a mission to be for us the *instrument of Providence and guide on the ways of faith*.

The house in Pietrelcina where Padre Pio lived before
entering the monastery.

Padre Pio's parents: Orazio Forgione (*left*) and Maria Giuseppa Forgione De Nunzio (*right*).

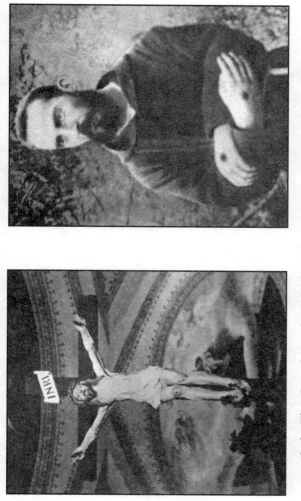

Left: The Crucifix under which Padre Pio received the visible stigmata.
Right: Padre Pio with the stigmata. This photograph was taken under obedience.

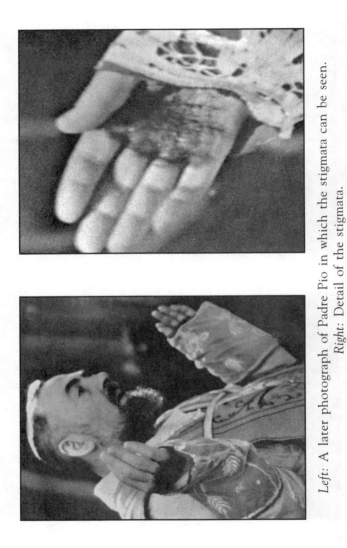

Left: A later photograph of Padre Pio in which the stigmata can be seen. *Right*: Detail of the stigmata.

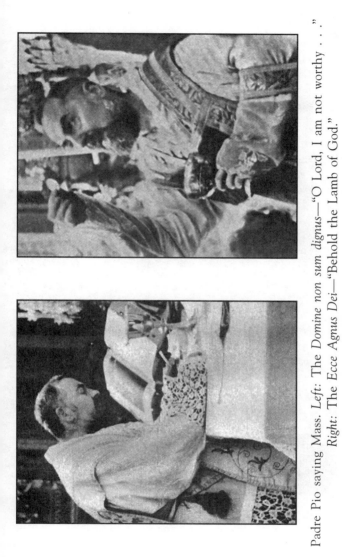

Padre Pio saying Mass. *Left:* The *Domine non sum dignus*—"O Lord, I am not worthy . . ."
Right: The *Ecce Agnus Dei*—"Behold the Lamb of God."

Padre Pio praying the Rosary.

Padre Pio hearing Confessions.

Madame Tangari speaking with Padre Pio in the sacristy.

Left: Padre Pio in the monastery garden. *Right:* The beautiful smile of Padre Pio.

85

"House for the Relief of Suffering." Padre Pio began this project to provide a hospital for the poor of his region. By the time of its completion in 1956, it had developed into a much larger work.

Padre Pio's last Mass, September 22, 1968.

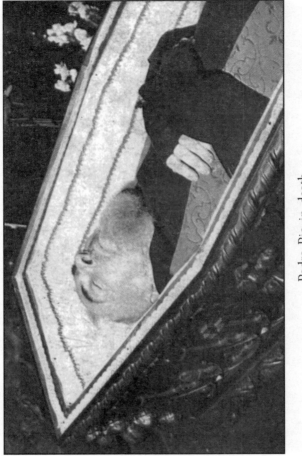

Padre Pio in death.
Padre Pio died on September 23, 1968.

Chapter 10

CONVERSIONS

". . . let us eat and rejoice, because this my son was dead and he has come back to life; he was lost and he has been found."

—Luke 15:23-24

In a certain sense, all of us who have heard the call to San Giovanni Rotondo and have followed it are "converts." It does not matter from what country or social background we have come, nor does it matter whether we were atheists, Masons, Communists, Protestants, Orthodox, or simply lukewarm or bad Catholics. All of a sudden, Padre Pio is there: he resembles a falcon that searches out its prey before bringing it to God. It is easier to follow him than to resist.

But what is a "conversion"? A conversion is a happy transformation in Christ with which we receive the joy of faith, fervor for the Commandments and love for the Sacraments. And with that we begin a new life that leads to our salvation, which Christ's fervent souls desire so ardently for all men. Padre Pio pointed out this way of salvation to innumerable souls.

Alberto Del Fante writes in his book *Per la Storia*, "I didn't hesitate to say that I was a Mason, an atheist; I didn't believe in anything. Padre Pio has given me life in every aspect: Today I pray, I hear Holy Mass every Sunday, I'm pleased when my children, before they eat, make the Sign of the Holy Cross to thank God, who gives us 'our daily bread.' Today I receive Communion and I am happy when God comes into my body. Whoever will have my courage will have my happiness."

* * *

All of Padre Pio's converts talk about this "happiness." Nestor Caterinovich, who once belonged to Russian Orthodoxy and after meeting Padre Pio converted to the Catholic Faith, along with his whole family, could not talk enough about this happiness.

"Padre Pio has triumphed over our hearts," he used to say to his friends with emotion, "but along with his triumph, he has gained for us such happiness that we can do no less than come to his monastery as often as possible to show him the continous gratitude of our souls."

I myself, in one of my first visits to San Giovanni Rotondo, remember having been surprised when a celebrated engineer from Milan spoke openly about the great happiness he gained through Padre Pio. After twenty-six years he had returned to the Church and the Sacraments, and without any human respect he told us how it had happened.

His best friend, a spiritual son of Padre Pio, had often invited the man to accompany him to San Giovanni Rotondo, but he had always refused. Whenever the engineer's friend returned from San Giovanni Rotondo, he said, "I have prayed for you and also recommended you to Padre Pio."

"You're wasting your time! I'm too attached to my sins," was the engineer's constant answer.

One day the friend brought him a little photograph of Padre Pio, which he put in his pocket only to please the friend. A few days later, when he was coming home from an outing, he sensed around himself a strong burning odor which he could not explain. He ran home, followed by this burning odor.

"What is it?" he asked himself, disturbed.

"Your extremely bad life," an inner voice seemed to tell him.

This thought, this sudden perception of the inner voice of his conscience, was to him as inexplicable as the burning odor that still surrounded him. Suddenly everything was clear to him: "I must change my life!" And, to his own astonishment, he told himself: "I have to go to Padre Pio!"

On the following day he left for San Giovanni Rotondo. He registered for Confession to Padre Pio but had to wait a few days. This wait for him was full of doubts and temptations, and he often asked himself, "But what am I doing here? What do I have to do with Padre Pio?" Still he stayed, and when his turn came, he made an excellent Confession to

Padre Pio with which, as he himself said, he received a new life and a happiness he had never before known.

* * *

Since it is not possible within the limits of one chapter to explain even the smallest part of the huge number of conversions obtained by Padre Pio, I will choose a few examples particularly well suited to give a better knowledge of Padre Pio and his priestly mission for souls.

MASONS

Alberto Del Fante, the writer and first biographer of Padre Pio, who by his writings led thousands and thousands of people to San Giovanni Rotondo, used to be a fervent Freemason. As a Mason, he had also written some harsh articles against Padre Pio in the Florentine magazine *Italia Laíca*, without even having met him.

However, a prodigious healing—attributed to Padre Pio's prayers—of Del Fante's nephew, for whom the doctors had left no hope, stirred in him a desire to go to see Padre Pio. He undertook the trip to San Giovanni Rotondo out of curiosity and with much skepticism, but when he saw Padre Pio and assisted at his Holy Mass, he was so struck that he changed his life; he went on to become a militant Catholic and one of Padre Pio's most fervent and zealous spiritual children.

From then on, Alberto Del Fante devoted his life to the propagation of the Faith, especially among his Masonic former brethren. His book *Dal dubbio alla fede* (*From Doubts to Faith*) aroused in many the desire to go to Padre Pio, and from him they more easily found the way back to the Church.

Not infrequently, Alberto Del Fante acted as a mediator between Padre Pio and his former brethren. Thus, one day one of Del Fante's friends, who belonged to the Masonic lodge of Bologne but had for some time followed with interest, Del Fante's writings about Padre Pio asked Alberto to have Padre Pio bless an image of St. Francis of Assisi, which the friend had been carrying around a while in his pocket.

Later on, when Del Fante went to San Giovanni Rotondo and wanted to get the image blessed, Padre Pio told him: "It belongs to a Mason, but a Mason who has St. Francis in his pocket already has the spirit of the Faith."

In fact, shortly after Del Fante had brought back to his friend the image blessed by Padre Pio, the latter wanted to go to San Giovanni Rotondo, where Padre Pio later guided him to conversion. From San Giovanni Rotondo, the man wrote back to his friend Del Fante:

"I am happy . . . I could not take a better step in my life than this; for that I thank you too!"

* * *

Dr. George Festa was the medical practitioner

entrusted by the religious authorities with the task
of pursuing research on Padre Pio's wounds. Later
on he explained the results of his research in his
book *Mysteries of Science and Lights of Faith*. He also
reported the extraordinary conversion of his cousin,
the lawyer Césare Festa, former mayor of Arenzano
of Genoa and one of the most eminent personali-
ties in Ligurian Freemasonry.

Dr. Festa had often described to his cousin his
impressions of his visits to San Giovanni Rotondo.
The doctor's opinions about Padre Pio's wounds,
which were scientifically inexplicable, and his admiration for Padre Pio were often the cause of sharp
arguments between the two cousins. One day, however, the lawyer Festa left for San Giovanni
Rotondo.

When he reached the monastery, he asked some
of the friars about Padre Pio, who himself happened
to be among them. Without waiting for the lawyer
to introduce himself, Padre Pio walked over to him
and, greeting him affably, said, "You, Sir, have come
among us, although you're a Freemason!"

The lawyer Festa, a bit astonished, answered
frankly:

"Yes, Father!"

"And what is your mission in Freemasonry?"
Padre Pio asked him.

The lawyer, with the same frankness, answered:

"To fight the Church from the political point of
view."

The rest may now be told by Dr. Festa, who

wrote some memorable pages about the conversion
of his cousin:

> There was a brief moment of silence, after
> which the pious priest took him by the hand,
> looked him in the eye at some length with
> limitless pity and tenderness and then, taking
> the lawyer with him, he began to tell him the
> parable of the Prodigal Son, putting the great-
> ness of the Father's mercy in such a vivid light
> in contrast with the moral misery of the son
> that the educated and intelligent man, who a
> little before had fought against my dialectic
> with the most harsh and violent battles in
> favor of his sect, wanted to fall prostrate at
> his feet, desiring only to hear from his lips a
> word of comfort, pardon and love!
>
> Thus, after more than twenty-five years,
> during which he had lost all touch with the
> Church, the Sacraments and prayer and was
> fed constantly by ideas contrary to the Faith,
> he was moved and happy and bowed down
> before the great majesty of that Word who is
> the joy and consolation of strong spirits.
>
> In the Confession of his errors, he wanted
> to impose on himself a complete renunciation
> of the false ideas he had pursued until then.
> In the Holy Eucharist, which he has since had
> continually in his heart, he began to acquire
> the energy necessary to undertake new, more
> moving and more glorious battles. Although

that day he had declared, along with a solemn abjuration of his wretched past, that in the future he would, with faith, follow only the teachings of Christ's Church, and although he had manifested his intention to officially give up his office within the sect at once, nevertheless, in consideration of the delicate tasks Festa had taken on, Padre Pio prudently suggested to wait until the Lord Himself, at the opportune moment, would show him the way!

From Foggia, Dr. Festa received the following letter from his cousin:

I'm coming back from San Giovanni Rotondo and I'm on my way to Genoa. Allow me to embrace you and tell you with all the strength of my soul: thank you! You have opened for me a road I am going to follow. I return with a profound sweetness in my soul, deeply moved and desiring silence, silence so that nothing may disturb my spirit.

In his account, Dr. Festa continues:

At Genoa, after this first episode, his life changed radically; he wanted to be in touch with the most enlightened priests of the city; he devoted himself to works of charity; he frequented the House of God assiduously, prayed, meditated . . .

Hardly a few months had gone by when he was here again, because he wanted to return to San Giovanni Rotondo. It was the first time we had seen him since the day I had maintained against him (and in vain) my last anti-Masonic campaign. With intense emotion, he told me about the wonderful transformation worked in his mind by the humble Capuchin of Gargano and showed me a pocket-sized edition of the Gospels on the frontispiece of which, before leaving, he had asked Padre Pio to write a few words as a memento. He read me these words, which express both the synthesis of his conversion and a strong warning for his future life:

"Blessed are they who hear the divine word with docility, keep it jealously and fulfill it faithfully!"

So he left for San Giovanni Rotondo, and after a few days he returned to my house. He was full of joy as he showed me the scapular of St. Francis. Padre Pio had wanted him as a tertiary although he was still in appearance a Freemason! When he returned to Genoa, he participated in the pilgrimage to Lourdes organized by the Archdiocese of Milan; he lived these days intensely, praying and spending his time lavishly to assist the many sick people.

This pilgrimage caused a violent campaign to be unchained against him. One article, published in the newspaper *Avanti!*, with the headline, "A Mason at Lourdes," caused alarm in the Masonic camp, which decided to call a secret meeting to take measures against the lawyer Festa. When he found out the time and place of the meeting, the lawyer made up his mind to participate in the discussions. The moment he stepped out of his house to go to the meeting, a letter arrived for him in the mail. It was from Padre Pio, who wrote him these inspired words:

"Do not let up, my dearest brother and son, in the pursuit of the truth and the acquisition of the Supreme Good. Be docile to the impulses of grace, following its inspirations and attractions. Do not be ashamed of Christ and His doctrine: it is now the time to fight openly. May the Giver of every good thing give you all the strength it takes!"

Any commentary, no matter how profound, would spoil the light emanating from this lofty document. I limit myself to pointing out that by a strange coincidence, precisely as Césare was going out to the meeting that was to judge him, Padre Pio, faithful to the clear promise he had made earlier, sent him the viaticum of his fervent word to pour into him, with ever greater vigor, the holy energy of the strong and to lead him to abandon for good the wretched sect that had held him for so many years! And Césare, animated by such powerful encouragement, showed up unexpectedly at the Masonic meeting. To the great astonishment of the people present and with serenity of argumentation, he upheld the greatness of the Faith of Christ. He spoke of the light of love which, with his mind's eye, he had seen springing from the humble and gentle words of the meek friar from San Giovanni Rotondo, and he declared that from that moment he intended to break off all relations with Freemasonry; in a letter he informed the Grand Master of his irrevocable decision.

He also wrote to Padre Pio to inform him of the striking episode that closed his life as a Freemason once and for all.

On the first Christmas after his conversion, Dr. Festa wrote with profound emotion:

On December 24 he was at Rome again. He came to my house and asked how I would spend Christmas. I told him quite readily that after visiting some of my patients I would go to Ara Coeli to assist at the ceremony of the opening of the Holy Crib. After he too manifested his desire to be there, we agreed to meet the next morning on the upper level. I thus had the unspeakable consolation of seeing him in the habit of a tertiary, together with other notable persons, accompany in procession the venerable image of the Child Jesus, with a lighted candle in his hand and his face betraying the most intense emotion in his soul.

Three days later, as he declared himself to be a lamb re-entering the fold who desired to meet his shepherd, he was received by the Supreme Pontiff, Benedict XV. Césare gave him a glowing account of his life story and the beneficial influence Padre Pio had had on his spirit, described his conversion, then showed him Padre Pio's letters. The Pontiff looked at them, rejoiced and exclaimed with keen satisfaction:

"Oh yes, Padre Pio is truly a man of God; some have had their doubts, but you shall contribute to making him known!"

In fact, the lawyer Césare Festa, as a fervent Franciscan tertiary and zealous defender of the Faith, contributed by word and example to making known Padre Pio's personality to others, along with his mission of leading souls to the Lord.

PROTESTANTS

How did we become acquainted with Padre Pio? How was it that Padre Pio, without leaving his monastery in the Gargano mountains, became known throughout the world?

It was Padre Pio's spiritual children and the photographs of Padre Pio that made him known almost everywhere. Every one of us came to Padre Pio through one of his spiritual sons or daughters; and before we got to know him personally, somebody had already given us a photograph of him, which made his face and his person familiar to us.

Above all, it was his spiritual children of the "first hour"—that original little group of grateful people who were either converted or healed—who led innumerable souls to Padre Pio with their words and example, prayers and writings.

This little group, which was around since day one, included an American and a German, both of whom came from Protestantism. As spiritual children of Padre Pio—truly good fruit from a good tree—they went on to become excellent instruments of Divine Providence for Padre Pio's mission.

Mary McAlpin Pyle of New York, who had once belonged to the Protestant Presbyterian Church, was led by Padre Pio to the Catholic Faith. Above all, she was struck by Padre Pio's Holy Mass, which made her decide to stay at San Giovanni Rotondo. At that time, the monastery was confined to its original solitude; there were no outskirts, no houses, no hotels or other places to find lodging. The inhabited areas were nearly a mile and a quarter away. So Mary Pyle's mother, once she saw that her daughter found all her happiness in living near Padre Pio's monastery, had a villa built just a few steps away from the monastery; this villa later became a welcoming house for everything related to Franciscan life. Mary herself became a Franciscan tertiary and dedicated herself to the development of the Third Order, which flourished in the shadow, or rather in the light, of Padre Pio's monastery.

Mary used all her talent as a highly cultured lady, an accomplished musician and multi-lingual person to serve the Church and the Capuchin Order. In her house, which among other things was the center of the *Schola Cantorum* of Our Lady of Grace Shrine, there were always many foreign visitors who desired to learn something about Padre Pio's life from this woman who followed him virtually from the beginning and could describe some moving episodes with a grace all her own.

Her greatest merit, however, consisted in the works she raised up at Pietrelcina, Padre Pio's birthplace. Through her indefatigable activity as a money-raiser and organizer, as well as her generosity, with which she wanted to offer even her own patrimony, she made possible the construction of the great Capuchin monastery with its novitiate, and the beautiful church dedicated to the Holy Family. Long ago, Padre Pio had predicted that a monastery would arise in his birthplace; Mary Pyle was destined to become Providence's chosen instrument for the fulfillment of this prediction.

Among other things, she took care to give the Capuchin Order the house where Padre Pio was born and the cottage in which he had spent his years of study.

In her guest house at San Giovanni Rotondo,

Padre Pio's parents happily spent the final years of their lives.

* * *

The German, Frederick Abresch, made Padre Pio's face familiar throughout the world. In 1930 he made the first photographs of Padre Pio. Mr. Abresch himself told me that his first attempt to photograph Padre Pio was unsuccessful. Without asking permission, he had tried to take some photographs during Padre Pio's Holy Mass. Padre Pio was quite indignant at this and Mr. Abresch, to his great surprise, found that the negatives were blank! However, he did ask for permission later on because he was not willing to give up on his intention to photograph the Padre. He did not get permission from Padre Pio, who was absolutely opposed to being photographed, but after much insistence he did get it from the superiors.

The photographs of Padre Pio immediately met with great success: they had a special charm and brought about some good wherever they went. Thus began the unplanned spread of these photographs, which eventually became a genuine apostolate for the good—possibly corresponding to a need of our time, which speaks to our sensibilities more with images than with words.

A foreign priest once asked me: "But how is it that he's always getting photographed?"

Padre Pio does not get himself photographed; on the contrary, it is no small nuisance for him to be surrounded constantly by photographers. However, because his superiors allow it, Padre Pio in his simplicity submits out of obedience. He has never had any fondness for his photographs; he takes a dim view of them, but he is often told that they do good, and he does not want to be opposed to that. One day, when Abresch showed him the photographs, he said, half facetiously, half resentfully, "Look how many Padre Pios there are here!" Abresch asked him to bless these photographs, but Padre Pio refused. Yet when somebody told Padre Pio that these photographs were bringing consolation to many, Padre Pio blessed them with these words: "Go throughout the world and do good!"

Frederick Abresch had a singular conversion, the history of which he himself wanted to spread in an ample account, which in its turn was published by Del Fante in his book *Per la Storia*.

I relate here the integral text of this account because it constitutes a truthful document that deserves to be known:

> I don't intend to give a complete exposition of all the things that happened to me, because I would have to write a whole book; but among so many I choose one, namely, my conversion, which I still consider to be the greatest miracle.
>
> In November of 1928, when I went to Padre Pio for the first time, it had been a few years since I had passed from Protestantism to

Catholicism, which I did out of social convenience. I did not have faith; at least now I understand that I was merely under the illusion of having it. Having been raised in a highly anti-Catholic family and imbued with prejudices against dogmas to such a degree that a hasty instruction was unable to wipe out, I was always avid for secret and mysterious things.

I found a friend who introduced me into the mysteries of spiritism. Quite quickly, however, I got tired of these inconclusive messages from beyond the grave; I went fervently into the field of the occult, magic of all sorts, etc. Then I met a man who declared, with a mysterious air, that he was in possession of the only truth: "theosophy." I quickly became his disciple, and on our nightstands we began accumulating books with the most enticing and attractive titles. With self-assurance and self-importance, I used words like Reincarnation, Logos, Brahma, Maja, anxiously awaiting some great and new reality that was supposed to happen.

I do not know why—although I believe it was above all to please my wife—but from time to time I still continued to approach the holy Sacraments. This was my state of soul when, for the first time, I heard of that Capuchin Father who had been described to me as a living Crucifix, working continual miracles.

Growing curious on the one hand, but distrustful at the same time, because it was happening within the Catholic Church, I too decided to go and see with my own eyes.

My first encounter with Padre Pio left me a bit cold, because the friar had only a few dry words for me, while I was expecting a warmer welcome, at least as a reward for the sacrifice of a long trip. Shortly afterwards, I knelt down at the confessional—God's tribunal. I will omit all the particulars and briefly describe only that which has a supernatural character.

Padre Pio made me understand right away that in earlier confessions I had omitted some grave matters and asked me if it was in good faith. I answered that I considered Confession to be a good social and educational institution, but that I did not believe in the divinity of the Sacrament at all. However, shaken by the impressions I had already gotten, I added, "But now, Father, I believe."

The Padre, however, said with expressions of great sorrow, "Heresy! Then all your Communions were sacrilegious . . . you must make a general Confession. Examine your conscience and remember when you last made a good Confession. Jesus has been more merciful with you than with Judas."

Then, looking over my head with a stern eye, he said in a strong voice, "Praised be Jesus and Mary!" and went over to the church to hear the women's confessions while I stayed in the sacristy, deeply moved and impressed.

My head was spinning and I could not concentrate. I still heard in my ears: "Remember when you last made a good Confession!" With difficulty I managed to reach the following decision: I would tell Padre Pio that I had been a Protestant, and that although after the abjuration I was rebaptized (conditionally) and all the sins of my past life were wiped out by virtue of holy Baptism, nevertheless, for my tranquility I wanted to begin the Confession from my childhood.

When the Padre returned to the confessional, he repeated the question to me: "So when was the last time you made a good Confession?" I answered, "Father, as I was . . ." but at that point the Padre interrupted me, saying, "Good, if you last made a good Confession when you were coming back from your honeymoon, let's leave everything else aside and begin from there!"

I remained speechless, shaken with a stupor, and I understood that I had touched the supernatural. The Padre, however, did not leave me time to reflect. Concealing his knowledge of my entire past, and in the form of questions, he listed all my faults with precision and clarity, also specifying the number of Masses missed. After the Padre had brought all my

mortal sins to light, with impressive words he
made me understand all the gravity of these
faults, adding in an unforgettable tone of
voice, "You have sung a hymn to Satan, while
Jesus in His ardent love has broken his neck
for you." Then he gave me my penance and
absolved me, and this absolution, which was
like a stamping out of my sins, produced in
me such happiness and a sense of "walking on
air" that as I went home with the other pilgrims, I behaved like a lively little boy.

I leave out everything else, even the impressions left by the Holy Mass, which gave me
the *coup de grâce*: I understood without further explanation all the mysterious grandeur
and beauty of the Divine Sacrifice.

To give a better idea of the Padre's greatness in Confession, I consider it opportune to
give some information, without which the
prodigious thing that happened to me might
be minimized. Humanly speaking, the Padre
could not know that I had gone on a honeymoon and that the Confession I had made
afterwards had been a good one; in reality it
was just so.

The day after my return from the trip, my
wife expressed the desire that we approach the
Holy Sacrament together and I consented. For
the Confession, I went to the same priest who
had prepared me for the abjuration, and he,
knowing that I was a new sheep and thus not

used to this, helped me with some questions. That was why I made a good Confession.

I wonder, however, who besides the Padre, who has the gift of reading consciences, could have been aware of these things? Only by virtue of particular gifts could Padre Pio make my Confession begin with what he pointed out to me, instead of where I had intended. As I already said, I remained in a stupor at hearing things I had forgotten myself; later on, with meticulous reflection, I managed to reconstruct the past, recalling all the details of which the Padre had reminded me with such precision. Critics and unbelievers cannot say that this was a case of mindreading because, as I already said, my idea had been to begin the Confession from my childhood.

To render the history of my conversion more complete, I will also say what the fruit of this happy journey was. Since that time up to the present, I have assisted at Holy Mass every day, also receiving daily Communion. I have become a Franciscan tertiary and so has my wife, and I believe not only in the dogmas of the Catholic Church, but also in the least of its ceremonies, and I think that, to take away this faith, one would have to take away my life as well.

I have given this account to render glory and gratitude to God and to procure peace and happiness to men of good will.

Mr. Abresch later had the great joy of seeing his only son—Pio—become a priest on September 2, 1956, in the Church of St. Dominic at Bologne. He was ordained by Cardinal Lercaro, and two days later, on September 4, Fr. Pio Abresch celebrated his first Holy Mass in the Church of Our Lady of Grace at San Giovanni Rotondo.

THE ORTHODOX

The history of the conversions that occurred in the Caterinovich family is from the first years of Padre Pio's apostolate. We owe the preservation of this history to Dr. George Festa, the medical practitioner and scientist mentioned earlier. Dr. Festa had known this family personally, and in his book *Mysteries of Science and Lights of Faith* he published a detailed account of these conversions written by Mrs. Caterinovich. It is a valuable document that may also stand in for many other histories of conversions which are unwritten and thus have not come to our knowledge.

Mrs. Rina Caterinovich d'Ergiu wrote the account after the conversion of her husband, which occurred five years after her own. The road traveled from October 5, 1923, the day of Mrs. Caterinovich's conversion, until July 6, 1928, the day her husband entered the Catholic Church, was a long and tiring one, in which the only stopovers available for recuperation were the visits to Padre Pio. Mrs. Caterinovich's account begins with her first

visit to San Giovanni Rotondo, in early October
of 1923:

I left with a friend of mine, who had been
a Catholic for a few years, for San Giovanni
Rotondo. We were living at Capri, where for
some years we had heard of Padre Pio and the
conversions and healings worked by him. I
belonged to the Greek Orthodox Church and
didn't believe much in living Saints and miracles. At Capri, however, I came to know an
Englishman, two Dutchmen and various
Protestant friends, who had been converted
by Padre Pio and were very enthusiastic about
him. My curiosity to know him became very
keen: I wanted to meet a real "Saint." I wanted
to see something "extraordinary." I was
Romanian by birth and a practicing member
of the Orthodox Church, but like all the
Orthodox, without real mysticism. For
although the Orthodox religion preserves dogmas which are akin to the Catholic religion,
in practice the priests themselves don't seem
convinced that we receive the living Jesus in
Holy Communion. Confession itself is only a
formality, which does not free the soul from
oppression and evil.
As early as when I had begun my university studies, I understood that I could not
believe as I once did, because the Orthodox
Church does not satisfy those who want expla-

nations and need intellectual enlightenment.

Because I had never been able to do any-thing without conviction, I abandoned reli-gious practices! However, before I got married, I had to go to Confession and Communion. I was at Rome, and the priest was a highly cultured person of the upper crust; I thought that in him I would find what I was looking for—explanations and enlightenment—but here again I was disappointed. That was my last Confession.

For eighteen years I did not enter a church or even make the Sign of the Cross, but at certain times I prayed, though more out of affection for my loved ones than in homage to the Divinity. Instead, I became interested in various spiritual currents. I read a lot and developed a passion particularly for books on Indian religion. It would take too long to go through the different stages of the spiritual life I passed over during those eighteen years. The War brought me back to God, but not to the Church; I still thought it was enough to live well, seek the truth and believe that God is infinite love—nothing more. When I went to Padre Pio, I was not thinking of becoming a Catholic, nor did I feel the need for the Church.

I had asked my friend to ask Padre Pio if I could go to Confession, certain that he could not refuse, but instead the answer was negative. And there I was, assisting at his Mass, during which a profound emotion overcame me, along with constant tears caused by the inconsolable pain of misery, my sins, and the fact of being outside the House of God. It was the pain of not having my true homeland on earth, and yet I now have two homelands here: one of them, which I love more than the other, is Italy, my spiritual homeland, and the other is Romania, which gave me life. A Catholic always feels at home, whether in the Far East, New York, or any other little town in the world where a Catholic church exists. This home I did not have; I had to stay outside the door!

When I was able to approach Padre Pio, I was struck a second time by a deluge of tears (I never wept easily before other people).

"Why are you crying like that?" Padre Pio asked me.

"Because I'm not a Catholic," I answered without willing or thinking it.

"And who is preventing you from being one?"

I explained some of my doubts, but Padre Pio said that doubting was useless, because the Lord wanted me. He gave me a little catechism and explained to me the prayers I would have to learn. He spoke to me simply, as if to a little child. When I asked him if I had to prepare myself by taking lessons, he said, "You must love, love, love and nothing more." It was October 5, 1923.

I did not feel and see in him what so many others had seen, but when I was near him, I felt more keenly the desire to approach Holy Communion. I felt that life without Holy Communion would no longer be life and that Catholics were fortunate to be able to have it, while I was deprived of it. I understood then that of all the Churches, only the Catholic Church is the one that really helps us to follow Jesus, to support us, encourage us and help us in everyday life.

Orthodoxy, on the other hand, no longer gave me anything. I had never understood, except at San Giovanni Rotondo, how far we are from Him who gave everything to save us!

I did not change my religion because I prefer the rite of the Catholic Church, but rather because, having a body, I cannot live only by the spirit, so I need help that only the Catholic Church can give; she is the only one that has preserved the spirit of Christ and helps us to follow it.

I spent the winter preparing for "the big step" in inner perils and struggles, temptations and trials, but always asking for Our Lord's help. In the spring of 1924, on April 10, I returned to San Giovanni Rotondo with my aged aunt who had raised me and with whom

I was very close spiritually, as well as my little daughter. On the 12th, I made the abjuration in the hands of the Father Guardian and the general Confession, and finally on the 13th I went up to Holy Communion, which since that day has become my greatest support, my strength and my consolation in the many trials and tribulations I have had in these recent years.

On that day the Lord granted me another extremely great joy: the unexpected and miraculous conversion of my aunt. She was a faithful, sincere and honorable individual, a woman devoted to duty and leading a very pure life, very tough on herself and on others. She was a diehard Orthodox and had considered a change of her religion as a lack of fidelity, a dishonor, a very base act. She had suffered much as a result of my decision (as I found out after her conversion). On the first day, she went to the monastery and spoke with Padre Pio, but she was shaken and disappointed by his words. She had been told that Padre Pio did not force anybody to become a Catholic, so when he asked, "Do you want to follow me?" my aunt answered, "No." She said that she understood that God is One and that therefore His Church must be one, but that she felt that her religion was very close to Catholicism, and she considered herself too old to change religions, especially since that would cause her relatives great pain. Padre Pio then answered: "Do you believe that before Our Lord you will have your relatives to answer for you?"

The next day my aunt did not return to the monastery, nor would she have gone back the following Sunday had she not received from Padre Pio, a few days earlier, a little picture with an inscription on it that had struck her.

After the Mass and my first real Communion,* very few people were still in church, and Padre Pio was in a pew behind my aunt, praying. Later, when he went into the sacristy, we followed him, and my aunt said to him, "Thank you for your goodness, and forgive me if I have caused you any displeasure."

"Not displeasure," Padre Pio replied, "you have caused me real sorrow!"

My aunt was struck by these words.

Padre Pio continued to talk to her for over a half hour, breaking down, one by one, all the stones of what had seemed like an unassailable fortress.

"The Orthodox Church is in agony," he told her among other things, and a little over a year later we saw how these words were verified, because the Orthodox Church divided into so many patriarchs and metropolitans!

---

*We translate the author's words as they stand, but it cannot be inferred from this expression that the Sacraments in the Orthodox Churches are invalid.   —*Translator*

It was a very hard struggle, but eventually my aunt was overcome; she was all shaken up and said, "I promise to enter the Catholic Church!" She kept her promise a few months later at Capri. Now, as if to make up for lost time, she is a most fervent Catholic and readily fights for her faith against all who are opposed to it, so much so that she has shaken up many souls by her example.

Within my family, my husband still remained in Orthodoxy. He was the most difficult to convert because he had always led a highly moral life, an honorable and laborious life, and thus he saw no need to change his religion to serve Our Lord better.

He was just as upright, sincere and intransigent as my aunt, if not more so, having been an officer in Russia's imperial army. He considered it dishonorable and base to betray his own faith.

When I decided to take this step, he was not opposed, nor did he discourage it; he merely made me promise never to try to induce him to convert. I did so, only putting him in God's hands, without speaking to him any further about my faith unless he asked. Meanwhile, however, I was praying continually and striving to correct my defects, to show him by example that my faith was better.

The essential virtues I was learning to value, which were totally lacking in the Orthodox

Church and in my life, were humility and charity, of which I had seen beautiful examples in southern Italy. Those were the virtues my husband and I lacked. My husband, who was very strict on himself, was also that way with others—to the point that he could not bring himself to pardon offenses received, just as he could not pardon human weaknesses, falls and miseries.

In September of 1926, I went back to San Giovanni Rotondo for the third time, and my husband wanted to come with me. No sooner had I seen Padre Pio than I felt a great devotion to him, a sense of tenderness and joy in being near him.

My husband felt as if he were in a state of isolation, just as I had, and during Padre Pio's Mass, he wept. He had the impression that he was a great sinner, that God did not want to accept him among his children, but later on, when he talked to Padre Pio about the religious question, he would not budge.

To my husband, Padre Pio was a holy man, full of goodness and love; he would have liked to be around the Padre all the time, but in spite of that affection, my husband was not prepared to act against his own conscience and heart. In the summer he got so seriously sick that he thought he was going to die, but St. Thérèse of the Child Jesus and Padre Pio helped him a great deal. Thus, in September of 1927, we went back once more to the monastery of Gargano, this time accompanied by our little daughter, and we remained there for several days.

Then my husband agreed to listen to Padre Pio give the reasons for the schism of the Eastern Church. He began discussing existing divergences with the Padre until one day, although my husband had wanted these discussions, he grew so irritated with them that he wanted to leave the monastery and return to Capri. In spite of my sorrow, I couldn't bring myself to oppose this decision.

Yet my husband did not leave, although he stopped going to the monastery until he got word from Padre Pio that, even if they could not agree about religion, they could still be friends. Then my husband returned to the monastery, and when we left San Giovanni Rotondo, his decision was already made: the only things left were the papers necessary for the formality.

When we got back home, a struggle began that was harder than ever, consisting of doubts, trials and unpleasant events that seemed like indications of Our Lord's displeasure with the decision. The inner struggles were tremendous, and in certain moments my husband, who was usually so good and affectionate, distanced himself from us and became like a stranger, sullen and cold. But the merciful Jesus did not want him to suffer any longer, and in July we went back once more to San Giovanni Rotondo for the great day! On July 6, he made the abjuration at Foggia in the hands of the Bishop, and on the evening of the 7th, he made his Confession to Padre Pio. On the 8th he received Holy Communion, and on the 10th he received Confirmation. "I want to receive Confirmation as a seal upon what has been done," he told me.

Thanks to the Lord, since that time he has been scrupulous in his religious duties and has been better in bearing with the trials that come from Heaven. He is also more charitable towards others and finds great consolation in talking about the Faith, which he is able to defend in his conversations with the Orthodox.

Rina Caterinovich D'Ergiu

I would only like to add a few words to this account of Mrs. Caterinovich, which her husband said one day to his friend Dr. Festa. They apply to everyone who has found the Faith, thanks to Padre Pio:

"Padre Pio has triumphed over our hearts, but his triumph has become our happiness!"

Chapter 11

FROM MY DIARY

During our stays at San Giovanni Rotondo, there were also little episodes and events worth recalling and contemplating, inasmuch as they too contribute to giving us a description of the atmosphere at San Giovanni Rotondo, so imbued with Padre Pio's personality.

I will take some examples from my diary.

Saturday of Passion Week
March 28, 1953

Today I was at San Giovanni Rotondo for my fourth Confession to Padre Pio. Although I was one of the last to go to Confession, I had enough time for everything I was supposed to explain and recommend to Padre Pio, and thus I left the confessional with a happy heart.

A crowd of the faithful was waiting in church for Padre Pio to finish the Confessions and come to distribute Holy Communion. I also got in line. There I remembered that I had forgotten my purse—which had my money inside it—in the car of my friend with whom I had come to San Giovanni Rotondo. My friend had left in the morning, right after Padre Pio's Holy Mass, while I had stayed at San Giovanni Rotondo for Confession, intending to leave later in the afternoon on the express train for Naples. Now, however, I had no money. Yet even though this was not a pleasant situation, I did not want to be unduly preoccupied with it. I was still too taken with the impressions of my Confession and wanted only to make a good preparation for Holy Communion. Besides, I could think about that later.

Meanwhile, as I was looking for my rosary in my pocket, I found a few hundred lire coins. They were not enough to cover the expenses of the return trip, so I decided to give them away as an alms. I went right away to the altar of St. Anthony and put these coins in the box for offerings, thus entrusting my return trip to Providence. And as if Providence had been waiting for just this little act of faith on my part, I received the assistance I was hoping for shortly afterwards in a completely unexpected way.

When I went back to my place in line for Holy Communion, somebody told me that a woman wanted to talk to me. In fact, far away in the crowd I saw a friend greeting me and giving signals that she was waiting for me. It was Teresa M., a dear friend of mine from Naples.

After Holy Communion, when my prayers of thanksgiving were over, my friend, who was quite happy with this unexpected encounter at San Giovanni Rotondo, said to me, "If you have nothing more to do here, come and have lunch with us and then we can go back to Naples together; there's just my husband and I, so there's plenty of room for you in the car!"

It was a wonderful surprise for me to find Teresa M. here, especially since neither she nor her husband were friends of Padre Pio. A few weeks earlier, we had had a discussion about Padre Pio, and Teresa had told me that she would not be going back to San Giovanni Rotondo again because Padre Pio had been too strict with her. That morning, however, her husband had unexpectedly decided to visit the Montecatini enterprises near San Giovanni Rotondo, and they felt that the least they could do was go also to the Monastery at San Giovanni Rotondo for a quick hello to Padre Pio. And here, when they had gotten into the church, Teresa, as she herself told me, had suddenly seen me in the crowd—precisely near St. Anthony's altar! I told my friend why I was there, and we saw in everything the hand of Providence. Teresa noted that such providential coincidences occur more easily in the vicinity of Padre Pio than elsewhere and that he had his part in them. She also told me that she wanted to be in touch with Padre Pio again.

As I reflected on what had happened, I thought: that is how we must give alms, without hesitation, without delay, without any preoccupation . . . with generosity and full trust in Providence.

Later on, we had the joy of seeing Padre Pio in a corridor of the monastery. We wished him a Happy Easter, and he gave us his blessing. As I greeted him, I said, "Padre Pio, thank you for everything!"

"What are you thanking me for?" he asked in his rough, frank manner. "Rather remember: he who does charity, finds charity!"

When we left the monastery, the world seemed more beautiful to us. Only then did we notice that the gardens and mountain slopes of San Giovanni Rotondo were full of almond trees in bloom, and only then did this view give us great joy.

We stopped for lunch, during which time we spoke about San Giovanni Rotondo, and then we returned happily to Naples.

San Giovanni Rotondo
November 9, 1954

Today there was not time to recommend all those who had asked me to explain their cases to Padre Pio. After my Confession, I only managed to place in Padre Pio's hands all the letters that had been entrusted to me for him and request his blessing for some devotional objects and photographs. After Padre Pio blessed everything, his glance fell on one little photograph, over which he also made the Sign of the Cross. It was the photograph of a group of employees and workers with their director, which had been entrusted to me by a dear friend, the director's wife, with great confidence in Padre Pio's blessing.

The reason my friend had wanted Padre Pio to bless this photograph was as follows: On the upcoming Feast of the Immaculate Conception, special ceremonies in honor of Our Lady were scheduled in the little city of S. on the occasion of the 100th anniversary of the dogma of the Immaculate Conception. The new statue of Our Lady, coming from Fatima, was supposed to make a pilgrimage among the households, and this pilgrimage was scheduled to end in the most important factory of the city—that of my friend. The personnel had already prepared the program of festivities, which was supposed to take place on the first Sunday of December, but their director, possibly out of human respect, was opposed to it and refused to give his permission.

Every attempt to persuade him had been in vain; that was why my friend had thought of recommending this event to Padre Pio and had sent the photograph. Padre Pio looked only at this photograph, and then he blessed it as well. This action of Padre Pio may have its significance, and therefore I believe it is a good sign for my friend.

First Sunday of December
1954

When my friend and his employees found out about Padre Pio's special blessing, they were certain the feast would take place, so they made all the preparations, although the opponent of the feast continued to refuse his consent. However, on Friday, December 3, one day before the beginning of the feast, everything miraculously changed. Not only did the director give his permission, but he even helped with the preparation, making no small contribution to the feast's success. Yesterday, Saturday, in the late afternoon, a car from the factory picked up the statue of Our Lady from the Cathedral to bring it to the factory, where it was exposed for the devotion of the faithful in a great hall on an altar full of flowers and lights. For the entire night there was a vigil before the altar of Our Lady.

This morning a High Mass was celebrated during which the director, his family and his dependents received Holy Communion. At the conclusion of the ceremony, the director himself recited with emotion the consecration to Our Lady.

In that hour, nothing came between the factory's foreman and his employees. In everybody there was the same joy; in many one could see that inner emotion which is capable of lifting hearts to God and lighting up the soul. Is that a small thing?

San Giovanni Rotondo
May 20, 1956

Today Padre Pio was particularly fatherly with me. When I told him that in some personal business I had been mistaken in some matters and would probably have to suffer some losses, Padre Pio asked me why I did not ask for advice in my last Confession to him. I answered that I did not want to bother him. Instantly, Padre Pio replied, "But you should have the courage to bother me!"

That statement, delivered with such frankness, delighted me: it was Padre Pio in a nutshell!

A PILGRIM FROM LOURDES

San Giovanni Rotondo
October 30, 1957

Today a gentleman from Milan said to me, "I'm here for the first time at San Giovanni Rotondo; I didn't believe it would be like this: all this crowd, this confusion . . .

"I'm used to Lourdes, because every year for the last twenty-eight years I have made a pilgrimage there. There's an immense crowd of people over there also, but everything is so well ordered; there's never any confusion at Lourdes. Yet here at San Giovanni Rotondo I actually feel disoriented!"

I answered him: "You're right; San Giovanni Rotondo could be confusing if you look only at the people and observe only the confusion, which for that matter may be observed sometimes but not always. San Giovanni Rotondo isn't easy for any of us.

"But stay here; go into the monastery, try to meet Padre Pio, stay there with him if only for an instant; ask for his blessing . . . and you will no longer be disoriented."

San Giovanni Rotondo
January 22, 1958
55th Anniversary of Padre Pio's
Religious Profession

Right after lunch I went back to the monastery again. A Capuchin Father of my acquaintance, who had just come from the refectory where he has a place at table near Padre Pio, told me, "A moment ago Padre Pio referred to his anniversary; he said, 'It's now a long time since my mother said: *I dreamed of St. Francis; he told me that I must bring you to the monastery of monks, because you must become a Franciscan friar!*'" Everything is that simple in Padre Pio's life!

He willingly speaks about his extremely pious mother and the fervor she had for his religious vocation.

San Giovanni Rotondo
May 25, 1959
Padre Pio's 72nd Birthday

"Padre Pio takes away our sons," I heard a mother say one time. "This is already the second one who's becoming a Capuchin . . . but that wasn't why we came to San Giovanni Rotondo!"

I remembered these words today when I had the opportunity to talk with a young man who had come to understand that he had a priestly vocation as he visited San Giovanni Rotondo. He told me that in January of this year, he had come here for the first time with his family. It was a visit the family had promised to make in thanksgiving for the healing of his mother. After this first visit, during which he did not have the opportunity to see Padre Pio, who was ill then, the young man kept coming back to San Giovanni Rotondo. In one of these visits, as he was praying before the high altar, he felt in an altogether

special way the living presence of Jesus in the tabernacle. It seemed to him in that moment that Jesus
had chosen him for Himself. Was it just a feeling?
How could this be so? he wondered. He was supposed
to be married in July!

On his way home, he felt an ever-increasing,
strange transformation within himself: without any
apparent reason, he had lost his taste for the world,
while a new and unfamiliar love was taking possession of him and making him happy. On Passion Sunday he was at San Giovanni Rotondo again, and in
that visit it was clear to him that without the Mass,
as he himself said, he would not be able to love any
longer and that now he had just one desire: to
become a priest so that he could celebrate Holy Mass
himself. He would have liked to talk about all this
with Padre Pio, but it was never possible because
Padre Pio was still very ill.

Thus, on that Passion Sunday, before the tabernacle, he made the decision to follow his vocation.
On his way home, he talked with his parents about
this decision, and as might have been expected, he
met with clear opposition, especially from his father,
who immediately suspected that Padre Pio had
changed his son's mind. In vain were the son's assur-
ances that he had never had an opportunity to talk
with the Padre. But the fact that the son clearly had
changed after visiting San Giovanni Rotondo was
evidence enough for the father, and therefore he
automatically put the blame on Padre Pio. So the
father decided to go to Padre Pio, together with his

son, for a clarification. They chose Easter Sunday to go to San Giovanni Rotondo, and this time a conversation with Padre Pio was possible because it was certainly necessary; it took place in the monastery, right in the Padre's cell.

"I have a bone to pick with you about my son, Padre Pio," said the father.

"And why?"

"In July he's supposed to get married, and now he has other whims in his head."

"What whims?"

"He believes . . . that he's called to become a priest."

"The only thing you can do is accept it, because he has a real vocation!"

Then, turning to the son, Padre Pio said, "Yes, you have a vocation!"

When the young man asked what seminary or novitiate he should choose, Padre Pio answered, "Go to Cortona!" (That is the Capuchin novitiate.) So Padre Pio gave them his blessing and sent them off with, "Go in peace!"

After this visit to Padre Pio, the father no longer opposed the young man's vocation; he was even happy that his son would become a priest in the Capuchin Order.

Today this young man has come to Padre Pio to greet him and ask for his blessing, because tomorrow he will enter the novitiate. Shortly before he left, he also came to us to greet us. He told us, "I can hardly wait to enter the monastery . . . I still can't believe that one day I'll be a priest . . . I should be going to Cortona on my knees!"

These words, spoken with his whole heart, made a deep impression on me. What a great transformation must have taken place in this soul!

The case of this vocation, which blossomed and matured in the vicinity of Padre Pio, goes together with many other cases of vocations, conversions and transformations that also blossomed and matured at San Giovanni Rotondo. In these instances there was no directly visible intervention by Padre Pio, although he undoubtedly played his part in these cases. In general, his influence over us was more indirect than direct; our transformations were more the fruit of his life of prayer and sacrifices than the result of his direct personal intervention. Yet whenever it is necessary, Padre Pio is also personally present, usually with a few words spoken with simplicity and singular intuition, to confirm and support the work of grace in us.

The way he acted on us was certainly not common; it had an efficacy derived from the fact that he moved in the domain of the supernatural in a surprisingly natural way.

Naples
June 20, 1959

The following is an objection from a certain Antonio, who had asked to come with us to visit Padre Pio.

"You know, Madam, that I'm very attached to our religion. And I really have nothing against Padre Pio . . . But I don't want there to be yet another Saint in the Church . . . It seems to me we have quite a few Saints already!"

"Antonio," I replied, "that's like saying: I don't want the wheat to come out of the ground this year because we already have plenty of wheat on this earth!

"Every era has to produce its Saints, just as every year has to produce its own wheat. Woe to us if we have not this fecundity of the earth and of our Church!"

San Giovanni Rotondo
August 10, 1960
50th Anniversary of
Padre Pio's Priesthood

Today the Father Guardian gave me back my missal, in which there is a dedication by Padre Pio.

This missal—an extremely beautiful Dominican edition—which I received as an Easter present, struck me as particularly well suited for a dedication by Padre Pio. So I brought it with me to San Giovanni Rotondo and gave it to the Father Guardian, asking him to explain my desire to Padre Pio. The Father Guardian would not promise me anything, and I had to wait patiently for a few months.

The fact that I got it back today, on Padre Pio's fiftieth anniversary as a priest, with this dedication, is for me a great joy! Evidently, even these little things have their own day, their own right time, in which they become even more lovable.

Padre Pio wrote the following words on the first page of my missal:

"If you want to assist at Holy Mass with devotion and fruitfully, keep company with the Sorrowful Virgin at the foot of the Cross on Calvary."

—P. Pio, Cap.

Chapter 12

LETTERS

Did it make sense to write to Padre Pio, who received hundreds of letters and telegrams every day and did not have time to read them? Perhaps in the whole load of daily mail, some letter, some telegram reached him; perhaps Padre Pio was asked now and then about a particular answer to be given; but these were exceptions, because the majority of the mail did not go through Padre Pio's cell. The correspondence was sorted out in the monastery by those Fathers who were given this office by the Father Guardian.

Although people realized or may have imagined that Padre Pio did not personally read the letters addressed to him, everybody constantly wrote to him! They wrote to him about their anxieties, their troubles and whatever was close to their heart. Often, very often, these letters were written in the most tragic moments, when all human hopes had vanished, when everything had been tried and nothing had been obtained. Then people would write to Padre Pio in a final effort of faith, to recommend everything to his prayers. I once read these words in a letter from a mother who, humanly speaking, had

no more hope for her dying child: *Ultimo Apello*—
"Last Appeal!" How many "last appeals" were
addressed to Padre Pio! And why to him?

It was Padre Pio's life, so intense in prayers and sacrifices, so permeated with the love of Jesus and Jesus
Crucified, that exercised an attraction on an infinite
number of souls; it inspired trust and hope, above all
in suffering and troubled souls, who instinctively saw
in him an instrument of God, whose job was precisely
that of helping those who needed it.

Not all were able to go to Padre Pio in person, and
it was not always possible to make the trip to San
Giovanni Rotondo; yet many, very many, moved by
the desire to tell him whatever was close to their
heart, wrote to him. For the most part they were simple, emotional letters, letters asking for the help of
his prayers, letters dictated by suffering. It did not
seem as if any of those who wrote to Padre Pio asked
themselves, "But who will read our letters? Who will
answer? Will profane eyes glance at pages written in
the height of our anguish, to criticize them or even
make fun of them?" No, those who sent their requests
to Padre Pio in the mail did not ask themselves such
things because they knew full well that it would serve
no purpose. They knew instead that complete trust
in the efficacy of the prayers of Padre Pio, as God's
instrument, could never be in vain. That is why they
wrote to Padre Pio, and if that were the case, it was
not without reason that they wrote.

Human sorrow, left to itself without any assistance,
can be fatal. Let us not pretend that those who suf-

fer are supermen of endurance. It would also be a mistake if we, in our own physical and psychological, material and spiritual well being, were to say to those who happen to be suffering: "Suffering is a grace! Rejoice that you have the privilege of being able to suffer." Oh, let us never say these or similar things to people who are suffering. As for this talk about the preciousness of suffering, only God can communicate it to the human heart without wounding it! Instead, we must, to the best of our ability, give help and assistance both materially and spiritually, to ease the pains and soften the sufferings of those who are wrapped up or indeed overwhelmed in their own miseries, so that they may find a way out, support, alleviation and, above all, so that a ray of hope may re-enter their hearts and rekindle their faith and trust in God's providence and mercy.

For countless souls Padre Pio's life of sacrifice represented the inestimable ray of light, the light of a new hope. This hope is able to reanimate faith in God, that faith of which Jesus said that it is capable of "moving mountains," namely, making the impossible possible. Such a faith strengthens, assists and consoles in every way and leads to graces being granted and to prodigies.

Yet it was not only suffering people who wrote to Padre Pio. There were also those who wrote him to express their admiration and gratitude for his priestly mission or to recommend questions of spiritual graces to his prayers—the right choice of a state in life and other important decisions to be taken. Still others asked him for prayers for their own parish, for religious communities, for priests and vocations, or they merely asked him to accept them as spiritual children.

And what about the responses? We know that Padre Pio never answered personally. We also know that a response did not come back for every letter that reached the monastery for Padre Pio. For a great part of the letters, the reply was a sort of little postcard from the monastery with a few "generic" lines that would serve as an all-purpose reply. Handwritten or typewritten replies dealing explicitly with the petitioner's subject matter were extremely rare. Thus, particular advice from Padre Pio was never passed on in writing from the monastery.

How then can we explain the continual flow, for over thirty years, of thousands and thousands of letters from every corner of the world, a flow which was never interrupted but continued and indeed increased constantly?

The explanation consists in the fact that if our letters were really written with faith and the right intention, they were never ineffectual. I can say this by virtue of my own long experience over many years, during which I passed on to Padre Pio innumerable letters from people who were suffering and sorely tried and needing help; I myself also passed on, in writing, my own needs and requests and those of others. In truth, Padre Pio did not disappoint us: in some way we were always able to understand that our letters had not been written in vain. The following examples might serve to give us an idea of this.

LETTERS FROM UGANDA

In October of 1949, a Comboni missionary of my acquaintance—Fr. Ercole de Marchi—was sent to Arua in Uganda. In his first letter from Arua, dated November 25, 1949, Fr. de Marchi told me he was unhappy that he had been unable to do anything for the mission, for just as he arrived, he had come down with a fever and was seriously ill. In his next two letters, dated May 15 and July 3, 1950, he was still lamenting this sickness, which was constantly getting worse, keeping him from any work or activity. I was very pained to hear this, because I knew with what fervor and joy he had returned to his mission. So I wondered how I might be able to help Fr. de Marchi, and suddenly the idea of writing Padre Pio came to me.

The experience of my pilgrimage to Pompeii in October of 1949, my general Confession and the extraordinary healing of my confessor in March of 1950, as well as my first very brief visit to San Giovanni Rotondo in May of the same year had stirred within me a great trust in the efficacy of Padre Pio's prayers and of his apostolate. Armed with this faith, I wrote my first letter to Padre Pio. It was a fairly simple letter, with words that concentrated on the essentials. I asked Padre Pio to offer a Holy Mass for the complete healing of Fr. de Marchi and to pray that Father would be able to resume his missionary activity immediately and do much for his mission in the future.

Almost immediately, I received the following handwritten response from the Father Guardian of the monastery: "We have received your letter with the offering for a Holy Mass. Padre Pio thanks you, prays for your intention and sends his blessing."

I was a bit disappointed. At the very least, I had been expecting two lines written by Padre Pio himself with some advice for Fr. de Marchi. At that time I knew too little about Padre Pio and what happens at San Giovanni Rotondo, and thus I felt disoriented, like that pilgrim from Lourdes who had been to San Giovanni Rotondo for the first time. Had I therefore written in vain? Was my trust in Padre Pio merely an illusion? What could I do now for Fr. de Marchi? How could I help him? Yes, I prayed for him, but I felt that these prayers of mine were too feeble to obtain extraordinary help for him. A case like his required prayers that were far more powerful than mine, and I had hoped in Padre Pio . . .

I sent the response from San Giovanni Rotondo in a letter to Fr. de Marchi, exhorting him to write to Padre Pio himself about whatever was close to his heart. This letter of mine reached Arua on August 9, 1950, and the next day Fr. de Marchi wrote a detailed letter to Padre Pio, to which he never received a response. Yet the same day he sent the letter to Padre Pio, Fr. de Marchi was delivered from the fever and from all illness. It was August 10, 1950, the day Padre Pio celebrated his fortieth anniversary as a priest.

Fr. de Marchi was able to resume his missionary

activity and went on to become one of the most active missionaries of that great and important region of eastern Africa, which is Uganda. As he himself wrote to me, he remained in the best of health in spite of the heavy labors weighing upon him.

Later on, when I had my first opportunity to talk to Padre Pio in person, I also wanted to recommend this missionary and his mission in Uganda to Padre Pio's prayers. One time, when I was afraid Padre Pio would be worn out praying for him, I asked him whether Fr. de Marchi could do something for him out of gratitude. Padre Pio swiftly answered, "Tell him to give me his Friday."

I later had a chance to talk about this strange response with a Capuchin Father who for many years had lived near Padre Pio in the same monastery. This priest told me that Padre Pio occasionally used to tell his fellow Capuchins, "Give me Friday and I'll give you the whole week!"

I wrote to Fr. de Marchi about this response of Padre Pio, and from then on Fr. de Marchi frequently mentioned Friday in his letters. In one of these letters, he wrote to me, "Don't worry, I haven't forgotten Padre Pio. On Fridays, which are often particularly troublesome, owing to excessive labor and all sorts of difficulties, I unite everything to Padre Pio's sufferings, offering them to God for his intentions. Sometimes I forget, but every Friday somebody reminds me to give this day to Padre Pio." In another letter he wrote to me, "On Friday, the cross is often particularly heavy, but at the same time consolations are not lacking. Just this Friday I received great assistance for my mission."

LETTERS FROM NEW JERSEY

An American acquaintance of mine from New Jersey sent me a letter for Padre Pio in which she asked that she, her husband and their children be accepted as spiritual children. The family had to make important decisions for the future for which they had a particular need for spiritual help and support. On January 22, 1958, which was also the fifty-fifth anniversary of Padre Pio's religious profession, I was at San Giovanni Rotondo. I had a chance to give Padre Pio the American woman's letter in person and explain briefly what was important to her.

Padre Pio told me right away, "Yes, I accept this family." That gave me the courage also to give Padre Pio a stamped envelope with the family's address and ask him if he would send some blessed images with a brief response. "Okay!" said Padre Pio; then he added, half in jest and half seriously, "What work you give me!"

Before long, the family received the blessed images from Padre Pio together with this brief response from the monastery: "Padre Pio prays for you and sends his blessing."

I had the joy of receiving the good news from New Jersey that everything had turned out for the best for this family; the family was able to make the right decision about the future.

"What work," in other words, how many sacrifices go in for every prayer heard! How many sacrifices by Padre Pio are transformed into benefits for us!

A TELEGRAM FOR VIENNA

Shortly before Easter of 1960, I found out that a dear friend of mine, who lived at Innsbruck, had suffered a heart attack while visiting her sisters at Vienna; she was in the hospital hovering near death. I was very saddened to hear the news and immediately wondered what I could do, how I could help this friend of mine. Whenever I have asked myself this question on similar occasions, I have always felt the entirety of my wretchedness and my inability to offer real help. Of course, I can pray. To be sure, we never pray in vain, even if we are conscious of the weakness of our own prayers. But in these kinds of cases, we need the help of powerful prayers. And because the sick woman's sisters also had great trust in Padre Pio's prayers, I sent the following telegram to San Giovanni Rotondo: "Padre Pio, we very much recommend to your prayers Mrs. N. B., who is seriously ill at Vienna, so that she may improve, have priestly assistance and go back home."

Almost immediately I received the response from San Giovanni Rotondo: "Padre Pio prays for the sick woman, sends his blessing and his best wishes!"

The response could not have been better, and it gave us new hope. In fact, my friend recovered from the heart attack almost immediately, and her health improved from day to day; she also had the finest priestly assistance and was able to go back home to Innsbruck.

And thus all three things I had asked for in my telegram, at a moment when, humanly speaking, there was no hope left, were granted to the letter!

Chapter 13

EASTER BLESSING

As is the custom in our parishes, during Lent there is a blessing of homes in preparation for the Feast of Easter. On the occasion of one of these Easter blessings, the chaplain who came to bless my home that year asked me to recommend to Padre Pio's prayers a nephew who was seriously ill. "He's a boy barely eighteen years old, who has come down with bronchial-apneumonia; there is very little hope of saving him, the family is desperate! Only prayer can help him, above all Padre Pio's prayer! Ask Padre Pio to pray that the boy may not die and that the illness may leave no trace." I answered that unfortunately I could do nothing, because it was impossible for me to go to San Giovanni Rotondo in the next few days.

After the chaplain left, I wanted to return to my work right away, but for a moment I took time out to look at my house: how beautiful it was after this Easter blessing! There was peace and joy—the beautiful gifts of this blessing. Everything struck me as being more beautiful than before: the order, the flowers and the thousand dear little items of my house. Yet suddenly, amidst this joy, I wondered: am I really unable to do anything for this family in distress? I did not know this family, their last name or where they lived, or even the sick boy's baptismal name. But so what? Somebody out there was suffering, and I had found out about this suffering; that ought to be enough to make me do something . . .

At first I did not know what I could do, so I lit a candle before the image of the Sacred Heart as a prayer for that family. By my own experience, I know how efficacious a similar little act of faith can sometimes be.

Later that afternoon I went to church, and following a piece of advice that Padre Pio had given me one day in Confession for a difficult case, I began a triduum of prayers before the tabernacle. Right on the third day, which was also Friday of Passion Week, I had an unexpected opportunity to go to San Giovanni Rotondo, and I was able to recommend the sick boy and his family personally to Padre Pio.

"Let them consecrate the house and the family to the Sacred Heart of Jesus!" Padre Pio told me with his usual simplicity.

When I returned and related this advice to the chaplain, to my surprise he told me, "You couldn't have told me anything better, Madam!" Then he told me that when his brother's family had gone for a long time without a house, they had made a vow one day that as soon as they found a suitable house, it would be consecrated to the Sacred Heart of Jesus. In the initial fervor of this vow, which had been made in a moment of extreme necessity, they had also bought a picture of the Sacred Heart, before which the consecration was to take place. Shortly afterwards, a very beautiful house was found that surpassed all expectations; the vow, however, was not fulfilled! The picture of the Sacred Heart was set aside in some forgotten place, and there was no further talk of the consecration. Granted, from time to time the chaplain had exhorted his brother to remember his vow, but the response was always that there were many other things to do . . . Thus did the years go by until that painful trial came, which was destined to lead to the fulfillment of the vow.

During Holy Week the chaplain himself, following Padre Pio's advice, made the solemn consecration of his brother's home and family to the Sacred Heart of Jesus, and since that day the son's healing began—a healing which was complete, because the sickness left not a trace.

Padre Pio teaches us to walk simply and naturally in the domain of the supernatural. Whatever he does is rooted in Jesus Christ, which is why it becomes so efficacious. Even from afar he can become for us God's supernatural instrument, and as such he guides us so that, from time to time, we too may become little instruments of God's providence and mercy.

Chapter 14

ADVERSARIES

THE LITTLE VOICES

"If you want to keep your devotion to Padre Pio, I advise you never to go to San Giovanni Rotondo!" That was what a friend of mine told me in 1950, when I confided to her my keen desire to become acquainted with Padre Pio personally. She told me about her first visit to Padre Pio, which was a real disappointment for her. Following the example of other people, she went to some lengths to go right up to Padre Pio, but he brusquely sent her away. Acting on her first impulse, she became angry at being treated this way, and she said out loud in the middle of the church, "If that's what the Saints are like, then we're out cold!"

Still, because she did not want her visit to be a total waste of time, she tried once more to go up to Padre Pio, who was at the altar. In her haste, however, she stumbled and fell clear down the altar steps.

On top of that, she was reprimanded by Padre Pio in front of everybody. She was so offended that she swore never again to return to San Giovanni Rotondo and to tell everybody about her disappointing adventure. For quite a while she was one of Padre Pio's most implacable enemies.

Adversaries of this kind were numerous. They would come to San Giovanni Rotondo out of pure curiosity to see what a "living Saint" looks like, or for some other superficial reason. When they did not find in Padre Pio the kind of welcome they were looking for, they were disappointed and offended and became enemies. Many of them would come back to Padre Pio sooner or later. With time they would come to know him better, and thus they would come to him with more serious, less superficial intentions. When they attached themselves to Padre Pio, something would change in their lives, which would become more conformed to the Church's teaching. With their Confessions to Padre Pio, they would begin to approach the Sacraments with greater frequency and devotion and easily discover those defects of theirs which were the real reason their first visits to Padre Pio did not turn out as planned.

There were also those who, although they would go to Padre Pio with good intentions, would not manage to obtain any spiritual advantage from their visits. Their admiration for Padre Pio smacked of fanaticism; they had a fantastic and thus mistaken image of him, an image that would necessarily be destroyed with the first visit, often by Padre Pio himself. The following case may serve as an example.

A friend of mine who was about to get married wanted to come with me to San Giovanni Rotondo to recommend to Padre Pio, in whom she professed to have immense confidence, some of her concerns that needed to be resolved. Fearing that my friend had built up too fantastic an image of Padre Pio, I advised her not to look for anything extraordinary in him, but simply to ask for his blessing and to recommend anything she felt was important to his prayers and his Holy Mass. My friend, however, did not see fit to take my advice, but did as she liked.

While Padre Pio was hearing Confessions for the women, she had an opportunity to walk into the confessional, and without saying a word she waited for Padre Pio to tell her something. She acted as if Padre Pio knew all about her difficulties, and so she waited for him to give advice and even some sort of revelation! Instead, Padre Pio did not give her so much as a look. Yet when my friend, in order to get attention, took another step towards him, he stared at her quizzically. Because she did not say anything, he asked her in his dialect, "What do you want?" My friend did not answer, and Padre Pio, a bit dryly, asked her again what she wanted of him. At that, my friend turned around brusquely and went away, visibly offended.

Later on in the hotel, she said to me, "You might as well know right now: not even ten horses could manage to drag me back to San Giovanni Rotondo again!"

I did not answer, and she, with great irritation, continued, "But it's unheard of! Never again to San Giovanni Rotondo!"

"Why?"

"He asked me what I wanted, while he should have

known that! I was expecting a good word, some good advice, but nothing of the kind! What am I supposed to do now? 'What do you want?' he asked me. I came to San Giovanni Rotondo to hear that? To be treated that way?"

"Perhaps you came here precisely for that . . . sometimes it's healthy for us to be treated that way. Our pride needs to be mortified."

My friend, however, would not calm down. "What an ugly dialect! I detest dialects; he should have known that too."

"But tell me something: why should Padre Pio have known all these things?"

"Because I didn't come to San Giovanni Rotondo to see a common Capuchin friar, but only because I had hoped to find a Saint here!"

"You got carried away in your fantasies, and in your pride as well. Yet I think it was good for you to have come here. You'll return to the reality of our wretched world in which there are not any all-knowing, all-seeing people, or living canonized Saints. But in this world there are many who pray, who offer sacrifices and mortifications on behalf of others, who have chosen the narrow and rugged path that Jesus pointed out as the one leading to salvation. Padre Pio is one such person. We ought to thank God for him and for the benefit of being able to come here from time to time, to draw new strength from his example and throw all our troubles into his prayers." Then there was a great silence between us, which I left alone.

A great many of these disappointed types would come back to Padre Pio; the crisis that had been brought on by the first encounter with Padre Pio was salutary for the most part. Even my friend did return to Padre Pio, although only after some time had elapsed. She chose San Giovanni Rotondo as the last stop on her honeymoon, and this time everything went well. She asked and obtained for herself and her husband the blessing of Padre Pio, who affably gave them his best wishes and said, "Always be united in the Faith, and try to be a family according to the heart of God!" Both of them were happy about this encounter with Padre Pio.

There is another category of people who belong to this group of "little voices," and whose name is legion: impenitent sinners, those who want to live conveniently outside of the laws of God and the Church and do not want to be disturbed from their comfortable life of sin. They are deaf to every call, every admonition. These people do not go to San Giovanni Rotondo and do not want to know Padre Pio. They sense instinctively that he is the implacable enemy of their life of sin, to which they are attached and from which they cannot extricate themselves, because they are stuck to it like flies on flypaper. They see in Padre Pio an enemy, and they combat him from afar.

The strangest things would sometimes happen to these adversaries: Padre Pio would suddenly enter their lives and would draw them to himself like a magnet, so that one fine day, without having willed it, they would find themselves in San Giovanni Rotondo. For a long time they would resist every appeal, and then something mysterious, inexplicable and stronger than they were would seem to intervene. The miracle of Damascus was truly renewed in this group of lost souls. It was precisely in their ranks that the greatest changes were proved to occur, the greatest conversions that nobody could manage to impede—neither the evil one, nor men, nor the world! And lo, from unbelieving enemies they became devout believers, from great sinners they became fervent, pure, sincere men! The once strident and malevolent voices were transformed into harmonious voices of praise and thanksgiving. Their happiness was immense.

THAT EFFICACIOUS "BEAR EVERYTHING IN PEACE"

Whenever I visited a particular shrine near Naples, I used to meet a Franciscan Father with whom I often had discussions about Padre Pio. At the end of our first meeting, he declared himself an "implacable enemy" of Padre Pio and told me, "We Franciscans in general have no sympathy for Padre Pio, but I have a particular aversion for him; I can't stand him!" I asked him the reasons for this aversion.

"Because he confuses people! How many fanatics and ignorant people have told me fabulous things about him; they have told me they're in constant contact with him and with his guardian angel and that they themselves, in case of need, send him their guardian angel . . . They call upon him day and night, as if he were a Saint; they go to San Giovanni Rotondo at the drop of a hat to question him as if he were an oracle . . . Is that good?"

"Father, as you yourself said, you're talking about ignorant people, and thus you shouldn't be surprised at how they admire Padre Pio. Nor is it surprising if they have a particular veneration for him, because even the most ignorant people perceive in Padre Pio a grandeur that isn't common to all. If this veneration often goes beyond the just measure and is full of exaggerations, it isn't Padre Pio's fault; if anything, their own ignorance is to blame. Yet their love for Padre Pio is a true and deep love that leads to something good. As soon as they begin to love Padre Pio, there is more faith, hope and charity in their lives; they no longer miss Holy Mass; they are more assiduous about frequenting the Sacraments and are more fervent in prayer. All we see are the thousand defects they have, while what God sees above all is certainly that spark of ardent love which has been kindled in their poor hearts, making them more capable of starting out on the life that leads to Him."

Another time we had the following discussion, which Fr. Gerard began with this question: "If I, in Confession, prohibited you from going to San Giovanni Rotondo, what would you do?"

"I would obey!" I answered.

"What? Then you'd be the first one to answer that

way. I put the same question to many of Padre Pio's so-called 'spiritual children,' and all of them were scandalized and answered that nothing and nobody could ever prevent them from going to Padre Pio. As you can see: rebellion! disobedience! And these are spiritual children . . . beautiful results! Don't you think?"

"I repeat, Father: it's the great ignorance of these people. Padre Pio is everything for them: they get attached to him as to an anchor of salvation. Padre Pio doesn't have the time to get into long discussions with them and convert them. So they remain in their ignorance and, unfortunately, in a certain pride as well, because they feel protected by him and want to depend only on him. They haven't learned anything from him, yet they're convinced that Padre Pio carries them, together with himself, to the desired goal. They latch on to his habit like street urchins do to the trams, in the hope that in this way they too may reach a good destination. And for that matter, Father, isn't it better that these people hold on to Padre Pio's habit, rather than to any old ruinous flag?"

The result of these discussions was that Fr. Gerard placed me squarely in the category of that "fanatical group of Padre Pio's followers," and from then on he never missed an opportunity to mortify me and show his aversion for me. Before other people especially, he never lost an opportunity to humiliate me, and if he was accompanied by other priests, he would designate me in the most ironic ways: "Here's one of Padre Pio's followers," or, "Here's the lady who's quite

familiar with the way to San Giovanni Rotondo," or
"Look at Padre Pio's Vienna-Naples branch!"

In fact, when I heard these "introductions" by Fr.
Gerard for the first time, I was a bit perplexed and
also somewhat offended. Yet because I had already
learned about that "bearing everything in peace"
from Padre Pio, I decided to apply it in this case too.
Thus, I stopped defending myself any further from Fr.
Gerard's humiliations, but accepted them instead as
if they were little gifts, something that gave me great
peace in my heart. I often marveled at this myself and
thought that Padre Pio must really be a great master
in the art of guiding souls. For, with a few simple
words, he used to succeed in changing our hearts—
which rebel so easily against mortifications and our
very touchy egos, in such a way as to induce us to bear
everything in peace, and with real joy and gratitude
at that!

A good two years went by that way until one day
Fr. Gerard came up to me visibly shaken and said,
"Madam, I have been waiting for you. Today I have
been waiting for you because tomorrow I'm going to
Padre Pio! I feel a call so strong that I must go to him,
and I would be happy to be able to go to Confession
to him. I know how often I have offended you, I'm
sorry . . . don't take it badly."

"It's nothing, Father!"

"Do you want to tell me something about Padre
Pio?"

"Gladly, Father!"

Then I told him about my Confession, in which

Padre Pio taught me that efficacious, "Bear everything in peace!"

GREATER TRIALS

It must be understood that in Padre Pio's life there were not just "little-voice" adversaries; there were also the loud voices of enemies and highly powerful opponents! The time of great trials, which had begun with the appearance of the stigmata and lasted for decades, was also precisely the time of the great adversaries who, like real touchstones, put Padre Pio's priestly life to every test.

This time of great trials can only be seen in the light of faith because, humanly speaking, it is difficult to understand. We know only that Padre Pio happily overcame the many trials of that period, concerning which only Holy Church, in the future, shall be able to give a valid judgment.

Chapter 15

PADRE PIO, SPIRITUAL FATHER

Since the day Padre Pio—in my first Confession described earlier in this book—accepted me as his spiritual daughter, I thought about obtaining this benefit for others as well. For I understood from day one that it is a real benefit to have Padre Pio as a spiritual father. Thus, I resolved to exhort those who used to go to San Giovanni Rotondo to ask Padre Pio to accept them as spiritual children. For those of my acquaintances who were unable to go to Padre Pio, I would request it myself in my Confessions to him. Right away then, in my second Confession, I asked Padre Pio if he wanted to accept my friend Maria N. as a spiritual daughter, and Padre Pio answered that he accepted her quite willingly. I then asked the same thing for another friend of mine, Rosa T., but Padre Pio answered me, "She'll be able to ask me herself."

As I was able to see, both replies turned out to be correct. For while Maria N. was only able to go to Padre Pio after some years, my friend Rosa T., after a few days, had an unexpected opportunity to go to San Giovanni Rotondo. In her Confession she asked Padre Pio if he were disposed to accept her as his spiritual daughter, and Padre Pio answered, "Yes, but you must learn to overcome your impulsiveness!"

This teaching, which was at the same time the condition for acceptance, made a lasting impression on her, for in reality she did often suffer from this inability to master herself, and she decided to follow Padre Pio's advice. Thus, the conversation that Rosa T. held directly with Padre Pio was useful and advantageous.

A few years later, when my friend Maria N. went to San Giovanni Rotondo and in her Confession to Padre Pio wanted personal assurance that she had been accepted as his spiritual daughter, she got this response: "But why do you still ask me? I already accepted you years ago!"

It was one of those answers typical of Padre Pio, who did not like to waste time in repetitions and always seemed to have been aware of the commitments he had undertaken for us. It was one of those answers that leave us a bit perplexed and make us see something in him that cannot be explained, yet which leaves us happy and content.

Padre Pio became for us the best of spiritual fathers. He guided us with few words or instructions, but above all by the simplicity of his example. He guided us in his own way. Whenever we really needed him, he was present to us with his inspired counsels, with his exhortations and with his prayers. And with his simple words, he was able to give us strength and assistance to overcome our difficulties.

WHAT WAS PADRE PIO LIKE AS A SPIRITUAL FATHER?

When we speak of Padre Pio as a spiritual father, we need to keep in mind that he was not a spiritual father in the ordinary sense. His way of guiding souls was completely different—indeed necessarily different—from the common way, because he did not have available the ordinary means and possibilities required for spiritual guidance. Thus, for example, Padre Pio was not always able to give us personal attention; there was not enough time for long discussions, conversations or instructions. Nor were we able to be guided by him in writing; only his very first spiritual children had the benefit of having been guided and supported by his highly inspired letters. However, after 1924, the ever-growing ranks of Padre Pio's spiritual children no longer had this benefit.

Nor was it always easy to reach Padre Pio: innumerable obstacles would come between him and us. Granted, we could use our Confessions to him to ask for his advice, but it was not always so simple to get to these Confessions, which for that matter were restricted to a very limited time, a few minutes. Nor was Padre Pio a preacher, who could guide us by his living word, nor a writer, who could convey his teaching to us through his writings. For decades he lived in the faraway, isolated monastery of San Giovanni Rotondo, and his days were spent exclusively in the monastery or in the church.

How then was he able to gather around himself a

multitude of innumerable spiritual children, spread throughout the world? Was it possible for him to be a real spiritual father for all these children? What was the basis for his care of souls? What means did he adopt? And what was the secret of his success? To all these questions there is only one answer: the real and proper source of his mission, of his apostolate, was his *intimate union with Christ*—above all with *Christ Crucified*—the union by which he lived and from which he drew all gifts for himself and for us.

His art of guiding souls was based solely on this union of his with Christ and upon the graces that flow from it. From this union alone he received the necessary means, and among these, in the first place, were assiduous prayer, absolute purity of life, intense participation in the Holy Sacrifice of the Mass—in which he always included his spiritual children—and the surprising constancy and fortitude in offering with simplicity, humility and docility his own sufferings for the love of Jesus and of souls. It should not surprise us that his care for souls, which rested on this basis and used such means, should have an efficacy all its own and be capable of moving with great simplicity, and quite naturally, in the sphere of the supernatural. It would instead be surprising if that were not the case.

One of my rather extraordinary experiences with Padre Pio as a spiritual father had to do with a decision of my friend who was mentioned earlier, Maria N.

I already belonged to the Third Order of St. Dominic, while my friend, notwithstanding the fact that she had become acquainted with the Dominican Order and its holy founder well before I had, had never been able to make up her mind to become a tertiary. One day, the prior of our Third Order exhorted me to speak with the friend and invite her to become a part of our religious family. I met with a flat refusal. She also had some trifling prejudices from which she could not free herself. Only rarely, therefore, did I return to this subject, but always in vain. However, since I knew about my friend's great esteem and devotion for Padre Pio, I thought about recommending to his prayers her eventual vocation for the Dominican Third Order.

One night I had the following dream: I saw Padre Pio in the chapel of St. Dominic in the church of our Third Order, giving Maria N. the white Dominican scapular. Although this dream had struck me profoundly, I resolved to say nothing to my friend because she had recently made it clear that she would not be happy about any "Third Order talk." But what was not my surprise when that same morning I got a telephone call from my friend. With great emotion she told me that in a dream she had seen Padre Pio before the altar of St. Dominic, handing her the Dominican scapular. The dream had been so clear that first thing in the morning she showed up in the church of St. Dominic, asking to be let into the Third Order. I then told my friend that I too had had the same dream, and both of us were quite happy.

Maria N. became a fine Dominican tertiary, and I took her as an example to imitate, for as soon as she joined the Third Order, she was always faithful to the recitation of her prayers. In spite of her many labors and family concerns, she never failed to recite daily the fifteen mysteries of the holy Rosary and the entire Office of Our Lady, something I managed to do only little by little and with great difficulty. It is above all due to her example and her exhortations that I love these Dominican prayers today and recite them daily. Thus, both of us enjoy benefits for which I think we have to thank Padre Pio.

As a confessor and also as a spiritual father, Padre Pio would guide us on the way of simplicity, purity and truth. He required of us fidelity in our religious, family, professional and social duties. He would point to prayer as the most powerful means of resolving life's difficulties. He would tolerate in us neither sadness nor discouragement, and even from afar he knew how to speak to our consciences, push us towards the good and offer us his help.

And what about us, his spiritual children? What was the mission Padre Pio required of us? What were the conditions, the requirements, the commitments that followed from belonging to Padre Pio?

Once we had asked Padre Pio to accept us as his spiritual children and he actually accepted us—for he did not accept everybody—our only commitment towards him consisted in trying to live always in a higher degree and in a better way within the Faith of our religion. We had no other duty, then, besides that which every Catholic has taken upon himself with Baptism. Yet we know that this duty, which ought to be the most important and natural one for us to fulfill, is unfortunately one of those things we most neglect. Indeed, we are always in need of help on the way of fidelity and perfection. This was precisely where our union with Padre Pio would be highly useful for us. In that union we found a good, an encouragement, a guide to correspond ever more to the requirements of our faith. For us that union was a support in difficulties and a help in the good we had undertaken, so that we could pursue it without wearing ourselves out and without mixing ourselves up; it would serve to free us from our lukewarmness and make us fervent. And once we walked onto the good road in Padre Pio's footsteps, the union with him taught us and exhorted us to love the virtues that lead to perfection and to persevere in this holy love. We knew that we must understand and follow the teaching of our spiritual father and have the good will to put it into practice and apply it in the actions of our own lives. For those who really had this good will and intention, Padre Pio, with his example and exhortations, was a wellspring of fervor, of trust in God, of patience and of that holy and wise simplicity that makes life limpid and full of peace. Then his prayers, virtues and sacrifices would be truly efficacious in every necessity and occurrence of our lives.

If we wanted to receive any advantage from being his spiritual children, our devotion to Padre Pio had to be, among other things, within just limits and never exaggerated or fanatical. Our devotion for

Padre Pio was not an end in itself, and thus we could not stop there. The end of Padre Pio was Christ, and therefore for his spiritual children as well there could be no other end than Christ. Padre Pio's real mission was precisely that of leading people to Christ. He was for us an expert guide on this way, which is never easy and upon which it is good to have somebody who knows how to guide, somebody who has precisely Padre Pio's experience.

Unfortunately, not all his spiritual children would profit from belonging to Padre Pio. How so? Ignorance and lack of religious instruction are often the obstacles impeding spiritual progress. Yet the true and proper reason must be sought above all in human frailty itself. Just as in every human enterprise there are inevitably defects and shortcomings, even so, here in the spiritual domain, human weakness has its part. There is, however, this difference: that every insufficiency in the religious domain is more noticeable than a multitude of shortcomings in other areas and is often the subject of harsher, more severe and at times unjust criticisms. For this reason, it would be unjust to judge Padre Pio as a spiritual father and the immense group of his excellent spiritual children according to the particular cases of his children—so unspiritual in reality—who did not understand how to take advantage of his teaching and example.

At San Giovanni Rotondo we would find several people in the latter category, and they would often make our visits bitter. By their anything-but-polite habits, they would bother the Capuchin friars, they would disconcert and scandalize the foreigners, and to the fervent, meek and patient souls they would often offer a chance to practice that virtue that St. Francis of Assisi, as a great teacher of life, called "perfect joy." Yes, for them especially, San Giovanni Rotondo could at times really appear to be the country of this Franciscan "perfect joy," which has the merit of being supremely beneficial to those who know how to practice it.

The union with Padre Pio was above all a union of prayers. Although it had neither formulas nor statutes nor special prescriptions, it was nevertheless a strong and useful union which taught many to pray and gave new fervor and new love of prayer to many.

Padre Pio, first of all, prayed, and he was a luminous example for us with his humble, assiduous, persevering prayer. Every day he would include us in his prayers, and he would invite us also to pray for him, to uphold him by our prayers and unite those prayers to his own. I will never forget his sorrowful exhortation in a moment that was particularly difficult for me: "Unite yourself to my prayers!" He did not tell me anything else, but these few words were enough to show me the way. I followed his advice—which really turned out to be valuable—uniting all my prayers to his for three days, and I was happily able to overcome those difficulties that had seemed insurmountable.

We could really obtain much by his prayers, but through him our prayers also seemed to be pleasing,

for often enough as a sign of thanksgiving and recompense, we received favors as a result of these
prayers. Thus, when Padre Pio once asked me to
recite for him three novenas to Our Lady of the Holy
Rosary, at the end of every novena I received a singular grace I had not requested or expected. The first
grace was the granting of a desire of mine which I had
recommended to Padre Pio years earlier, but which,
over time, I had given up on. The second grace had
to do with a favor that I had one day entrusted to
Padre Pio's prayers, but I had ceased thinking about,
considering it impossible to obtain. The third grace
consisted in help that reached me at the right
moment in a particular necessity. Another time,
when I found myself in grave danger during a trip, I
promised to recite for Padre Pio an entire Rosary
before the tabernacle if I escaped. Almost as soon as
I made this promise, I was saved from the danger, and
I was able to fulfill the promise that same evening.

The union with Padre Pio undoubtedly makes it
easier for our prayers—and both the great and small
desires we hold close to our heart—to be granted. We
may be grateful for that, but we should not see the
meaning of such a union as consisting in that alone.
The union of those who pray a community of prayers
may only have meaning if it goes beyond the confines
of our own interests, to be useful to many. Every community of prayers is a power that has within itself
immense force to spread good in the world, by which
it lessens human suffering, makes up for human
faults, obtains conversions, raises up holy vocations

and conveys peace, along with spiritual and material wellbeing to a multitude of souls.

In truth, the first step we take towards such a community almost always has a personal motive; our own sufferings and troubles are in fact what move us to look for help. The first prayers are then addressed for ourselves, and at first we don't even see anything before us other than our own troubles, from which we seek to be delivered, and our problems, which we want to see resolved. That is not a bad thing. Fortunate are those who in the unpleasant situations of life have recourse to the means offered by the Faith and who take refuge in prayer rather than give themselves up to despair.

Thus, it is a good thing if our necessities move us towards the good way of faith and are our initial motive for beginning a more intense life of prayer. In this way we may experience for ourselves the power of prayer, and as we gradually resolve our problems, a new order, a new well-being shall enter our life; the hearing of our prayers shall be for us a source of consolation and joy, strengthening the faith in us, urging us to spread this good way and also to recommend it to others. Little by little the circle will become wider, because we are always learning increasingly to include the needs of others in our prayers. Before long there will no longer be strangers for us but only brethren, and no distances will exist that cannot be bridged by our prayers, because wherever there are human sufferings, there will always be our prayers. All the necessities of our dear ones, our friends and acquaintances, our parishes, our Order, our country and the whole Church shall be included in our prayers. Let us pray for priests, for vocations, for the sick, for prisoners, for all those who are wrapped up in the miseries of life. Let us pray for those who do not believe, so that they may reach the Faith, and let us pray for the fervent, that they may remain in their fervor. Let us pray for the Church of silence, for our enemies, for all those who do not pray. Let us embrace with our prayers all of humanity, the whole world! This is why we are called Catholic.

Union with Padre Pio can be for us a precious encouragement and a particularly useful school on this road.

Chapter 16

THE WORKS OF PADRE PIO

When we speak about the works of Padre Pio, what comes to our mind right away is that enormous work that came from San Giovanni Rotondo which Padre Pio wanted to call the "House for the Relief of Suffering."

Initially, Padre Pio's intention had merely been to give the poorest people of that part of Gargano a hospital where they could recuperate and be cared for in case they got sick. At that time, in that entire vast region of Gargano, there was not a hospital able to take in the sick of that region. The population was made up almost exclusively of shepherds and agricultural workers who were particularly tried by almost inhuman misery and who almost nobody had thought of assisting up until then. Padre Pio was the first to be moved by this misery and to think of remedying it with powerful assistance. Padre Pio's first motive, then, for taking up this work was compassion towards those who were forgotten by all; his first intention was to soften their pains, to give relief to the most forgotten suffering souls. That was why Padre Pio wanted to give his work this title, which will include within itself for all time his original intention.

It was undoubtedly a daring thought that projected this work. Yet after Padre Pio was delivered in 1939 from restrictions that had been imposed on him in 1923, he wanted to dedicate himself with commitment to the realization of the projected enterprise.

During January of 1940, in his cell and in the presence of other people, the decision to found the hospital was taken.

The beginnings were rather modest: Padre Pio himself offered the first little nest egg, and his example was then followed by his friends, who among other things wanted to offer their free co-operation. Thus, a doctor from Florence, a construction man from the Abruzzi Mountains and an accountant from Zara were the first volunteers for Padre Pio's work.

The first little offerings to arrive from the outside were recorded in a common school notebook and scrupulously administered. Although Padre Pio had not been able to publicize his work, it quickly became known all over, and ever more generous offerings miraculously flowed in. News about the work just conceived by Padre Pio even reached America and especially touched the hearts of people who had left the regions of the Gargano Mountains; these regions had been too poor to yield bread to all, so the emigrants went to earn their living in the distant lands of America. From these emigrants, the work received many contributions. It was also a son of the poor Gargano Mountain region who gave Padre Pio the greatest assistance: Fiorello La Guardia, who, when Padre Pio began his work, happened to be mayor of New York and president of the charitable organization UNRRA. He made enough money available to assure the work's financial basis. And this was the cause of even greater works, because as a result of the generous donation, the original idea of creating a little hospital for local use was abandoned, and it was decided to construct a far more generous work for the benefit of all the sick, regardless of where they came from.

The work was begun after the War, in May of 1947. Nine years later, in May of 1956, the great hospital was ready to be inaugurated by Padre Pio in the presence of ecclesiastical and civil authorities and an immense crowd of the faithful. Padre Pio's House for the Relief of Suffering became one of Europe's most modern hospitals, with over a thousand beds arranged in spacious rooms, with all the modern comforts. Padre Pio did not want his sick to lack anything.

Next to the great hospital there are buildings for administration and residences for the doctors, sisters and nurses. Spacious alleys surrounded by well-kept gardens lead to the hospital and the adjacent offices, giving the whole complex a generous and welcoming appearance.

We see and admire the beauty and greatness of this work, which has given limitless benefits to thousands and thousands of sick people and has become an important center of modern medical science. What we do not see are the innumerable sacrifices and many sufferings that Padre Pio had to undergo for it. We see only the glory that the work seems to have brought its founder, but we do not see the troubles it cost him.

Upon Padre Pio's cell, the very one where the now grandiose work found its humble beginnings, an inscription taken from the *Imitation of Christ* was written. It seems almost prophetic: "The glory of the world is always accompanied by sorrow."

Along with this great social and charitable work, other works arose, which were the natural and necessary consequences of the first one. The very first blow of the spade, initiating the labors for the construction of Padre Pio's hospital, had a vast echo throughout the Gargano region. This mountainous, bare and impoverished region—one side of which rises alongside the highly fertile plains of Puglia, and the other of which faces the blue waves of the Adriatic Sea—had been one of the most inhospitable areas. Its rocky ground was unwelcoming to trees or any sort of agricultural produce and offered only the stingiest possibility of a livelihood. If there were any thought of building homes or roads, the necessary room could be freed up only by dynamiting the stone boulders. And lo and behold, this area, which had once been so stingy with its gifts that it could not even give bread to its children, this land which was considered so worthless that nobody even wanted to own it, showed how valuable it really was, thanks to the labors begun at San Giovanni Rotondo for Padre Pio's works! In fact, the work over the vast construction site caused the discovery of the inner riches of the soil, which is full of metals, bauxite and marble, and is now among the most highly valued ground in Italy.

Another immediate consequence of the work at San Giovanni Rotondo was the construction of the beautiful highways that go up from the plains of Puglia to areas in the Gargano Mountains. A well regulated bus service makes San Giovanni Rotondo easily accessible. Everywhere there is new life: the ancient little center of San Giovanni Rotondo, which was once about a mile and a quarter from the monastery, has now grown and extends clear to the monastery, with modern homes, beautiful villas with their gardens, boarding houses and hotels. The hotels arose in order to offer a dignified welcome to the countless visitors coming from all over the world. That was criticized by some, but anybody familiar with the life led in San Giovanni Rotondo can well appreciate this attempt to give the area good hotels and give the ever growing ranks of visitors the benefit of a dignified atmosphere corresponding to modern life's spiritual and material demands.

At the time Mary Pyle came to San Giovanni Rotondo—around 1930—in the vicinity of the monastery there were only caves, where the shepherds and their flocks found refuge. During my first visit in 1950, I found only a sort of inhospitable boarding house, which had no running water, no lights or plumbing, and left the worst impression on us all. Many visitors had to spend the night in the open air or share makeshift dormitories and even beds with others. In the long run, such a state of negligence could not be tolerated, and so the decision was finally made to build hotels furnished with all the modern comforts.

Since 1959, the large and beautiful Church of Our Lady of Grace has also existed alongside the ancient little monastery church. The construction of this great church was an urgent necessity also, because over time the old little church ceased to be sufficient to receive all the faithful. This work also must be categorized among those works which would not have arisen without Padre Pio and which represent the practical activity of his priestly mission. Around Padre Pio there is never room for inertia, there is never idleness; around him there is always bread and work for all. And that is a social work of no small importance!

Padre Pio's second great work arose in the area where he was born, Pietrelcina. It is the Capuchin monastery with its adjacent church.

With the House for the Relief of Suffering at San Giovanni Rotondo, Padre Pio gave something to the world. With the monastery and church of Pietrelcina, Padre Pio gave something to his Order.

This second work was built in the postwar period. When construction of the House for the Relief of Suffering began in 1947, the Monastery of Pietrelcina was virtually finished, while the beautiful, spacious church dedicated to the Holy Family was inaugurated in 1953.

San Giovanni Rotondo appears totally changed through Padre Pio's works: the so-called "Kingdom of Shepherds," as it was once known, has been transformed into a city with an entirely modern look.

Pietrelcina, on the other hand, has kept its previous appearance: it has remained as it was, a humble little agricultural area in the hills of Benevento, with its cobblestone streets and distinctive staircases, overlooked by rustic houses and the little terraces of old churches. Everything there is made of stone, as if to give visible confirmation to its name.* Between the houses there are little stone terraces and miniature gardens, equally surrounded by stone, in which a single fig tree can often be seen—a tree which, owing to its rich harvest, is of no small importance in the family budget.

Here in this little area, where life still has its own rhythm and is not dominated by the fast pace of the modern world, where it would not be surprising to meet, in one of its silent old streets, St. Francis of Assisi on the way with his brethren—here Padre Pio had predicted that one day a great monastery and a new church would arise.

During his first few years of study, when he was still at Pietrelcina, Padre Pio was on one of his usual walks one evening together with the archpriest Don Salvatore. Padre Pio stopped before a site where a monastery had existed long ago. At that moment the bells of Pietrelcina rang the Angelus and Padre Pio said, "The echo of these bells reminds me of another bell, that of the former monastery, and makes me think that another more beautiful and larger one must arise.

------

*The author is of course referring to the fact that "Pietrelcina" is derived from "pietra," "stone."—*Translator*.

"And when will this come to pass?" the archpriest asked him.

"I don't know," Padre Pio answered. "I can't say, but I think it will happen."

Thirty years later, his prediction became reality, and upon the site of the old monastery "another more beautiful and larger one" arose.

Although Padre Pio was not able to do anything personally for the practical accomplishment of the work of Pietrelcina, this too is his work and his work alone. For there is not a stone or a window or a pew or an altar in this church or monastery which is not the fruit of devoted and grateful offerings to Padre Pio from his spiritual children, including, in the first place, those who emigrated from Pietrelcina to America. Padre Pio did not even ask any of us to help in the fulfillment of this work, yet many were filled with such fervor for it that they happily contributed with their own offerings and with collections taken from among their acquaintances, so that the monastery and church were finished in a relatively short time. The true and proper instrument chosen by Providence for the works of Pietrelcina, however, was Mary Pyle, who dedicated herself to them indefatigably and, by her example, imparted fervor to others.

The Monastery and Church of the Holy Family at Pietrelcina are today a luminous center of faith, which welcomes new Capuchin vocations and unites around itself the faithful of the Franciscan Third Order. Padre Pio truly could not have given a more beautiful gift to his place of birth.

Chapter 17

THE WRITINGS OF PADRE PIO

Padre Pio's writings are limited to some meditations and to a number of letters written between the years 1914 and 1924 to his first spiritual children. They are beautiful letters, full of precious advice that shed light on the entirety of Padre Pio's care for the salvation of those souls whom Divine Providence chose to entrust to his priestly care.

After 1924, there were no longer any letters nor other writings of Padre Pio, because in that year, along with some other restrictions, he was prohibited from writing. Yet even during this long period of not writing, Padre Pio has given us a precious page: that of his example! His unconditional obedience, his humble acceptance of whatever bitter things religious life might have offered him, and his faithfulness in pursuing his duties without bothering about his own sufferings can be priceless teachings for us all.

As is well known, in 1939 Padre Pio was freed from the restrictions of the years 1923-24; the only one that remained was the one about writing, and that was out of consideration for his stigmata, which made it painful. Thus, even after 1939, we have no other writings of Padre Pio.

As for the meditations, Padre Pio wrote them only for himself, not ever suspecting that they would be published one day. Of these meditations, two are particularly well known, thanks to Fr. Ezechia Cardone, O.F.M., who took care of their publication, with the approval of ecclesiastical authority, during the years 1952-1954. The first one is entitled *The Agony of Jesus in the Garden*, and the second one is called *Prayer In Honor of the Immaculate Conception.* * The former was especially widespread, and many used it for recitation of the Holy Hour. It is a beautiful meditation that puts in clear relief Padre Pio's intense love for the suffering Jesus, whom he followed step by step during his bitter Passion in the hours of Gethsemane. By his warm words and his loving compassion, Padre Pio really does succeed in leading us very close to Jesus in the Garden of Olives.

---

*These two brief works have been published by TAN as *The Agony of Jesus* and *Meditation Prayer on Mary Immaculate.* —*The Publisher*, 1996.

Chapter 18

THE MONASTERY OF OUR LADY OF GRACE

FRAGMENTS OF THE MONASTERY'S HISTORY

The history of Our Lady of Grace Monastery in San Giovanni Rotondo certainly would have been hidden in silence except that for decades the monastery's harmonious name has been associated with another name known throughout the world: Padre Pio.

In one of my visits to San Giovanni Rotondo, a Capuchin Father from the monastery lent me an old document containing the chronicle of the monastery. From this document I have drawn the dates and information about the most important stages in its humble history.

At the beginning of the sixteenth century, San Giovanni Rotondo became an important commercial center for the areas dispersed over the Gargano mountains and for the neighboring cities of Puglia; there was some thought then about giving the people adequate religious assistance. For this purpose the religious of the Capuchin Order were chosen, and with this choice also began the history of Our Lady of Grace Monastery.

It was Cardinal Giammaria of Monte San Sabino—who later became Pope Julius III—who called the Capuchins to San Giovanni Rotondo, favored their mission near the people and finally authorized the foundation of the monastery.

The Capuchin friars were thus invited by the Cardinal to choose for themselves the site most suitable for building the monastery. A cheerful and healthy site was chosen at the foot of the mountains, in a beautiful solitude about a mile and a quarter from any settlement. Here a certain Orazio Antonio Landi had a vineyard and a rural cottage which he generously gave the friars.

In 1540, a cross was erected on this hillock, as we read in the old chronicle, "and the brethren raised the monastery walls to the summit of the hill, in full view of that area, by the will of the people, who with such great emulation tried to extend a helping hand in the erection of the edifice." Next to the monastery a little church arose, dedicated to Our Lady of Grace.

"In this hermitage," the chronicler writes, "the religious strove fervently to acquire the holy virtues, and especially holy poverty, because they well knew what our Seraphic Father had said: that poverty makes us poor in possessions but enriches us with virtues. And why be afraid of want, if we have for our provider the God of Heaven and earth? Oh, what beatitude it was for them to pay attention only to heavenly things, depending for everything else on the Lord's loving providence, which did not fail to provide them with the necessary sustenance, even in a miraculous way, as we see in fact in the year 1548 . . ."

In fact, it is related in part one of the first volume of the annals of the monastery that enough snow fell that year to isolate the monastery completely, making it impossible for the brother entrusted with alms collecting to provide for the needs of his fellow brothers. Already all the bread and legumes were gone, and as there was no hope of human assistance, the friars had recourse to the Lord. That same evening, "four young men of lordly appearance came to the monastery, one with bread, the other with wine, and the third and fourth with various kinds of foods. And because there was not anybody in the monastery who knew them, the doorkeeper asked them whence they had come from and who had sent the alms, so that the brothers could then give the proper thanks. Yet the young men only said, "Thank the Lord, who does not abandon his faithful servants in their needs!" And thus they suddenly left.

After a few days, the local people were amazed that the friars had not come for the usual alms. They suspected that the brothers had been impeded by the snow and were in the utmost need. So they sent some men who opened a path through the snow and got to the monastery. They learned from the brethren that some days earlier they had been in distress, but then they had been assisted by the devotion of four young men and had been saved from dire need. The messengers returned to report what had happened to those who had sent them, and in spite of a diligent inquiry to discover the identity of the pious benefactors, they were utterly unable to locate the youths. The people understood that it was not possible for such an alms to have come from other localities, which were quite distant; besides, the snow had been very high. So they recognized the miracle and were convinced that it had been Angels who, in the form of young men, had provided for the needs of the poor volunteers of Jesus Christ. So all of them together made a promise that whenever the snow rose higher than the length of the palm of a hand, the people at their own expense would provide whatever the Capuchins needed by way of food.

The Holy Year 1575 signaled a new extraordinary event for the Monastery at San Giovanni Rotondo: the first encounter with God of a soul chosen for sanctity. In fact, right here in the little Monastery of Our Lady of Grace, the prodigious conversion of St. Camillus de Lellis began.

In January of that year, young Camillo de Lellis, who was then in the service of the Capuchin Fathers of Manfredonia, was given the task of going over to the friars of San Giovanni Rotondo to pick up some wine. During his brief stay in the Monastery of Our Lady of Grace, he was profoundly struck by a conversation he had with the Father Guardian, whose inspired words had a decisive importance for his future. On the following day—February 2, 1575, the Feast of the Purification—he first commended himself to the pious friar's prayers and then left the monastery in the early morning hours to return to Manfredonia. It was on that lonely road, shortly after he had left the Monastery of Our Lady of Grace, that Camillus felt God's call even more intensely, and like St. Paul on the road to Damascus, he decided to follow it with all his heart. It was a great conversion, which totally changed his life, leading him on the way to his true vocation; Camillus became the founder of a religious order and a Saint. As a Saint, he went on to bring into the world the sign of the Red Cross, which became the symbol of Christian charity for all humanity. As a result, St. Camillus of Lellis is also known as the father of the Red Cross.

Not everybody knows the origin of the Red Cross, and only a few people know that we owe it to the conversion of St. Camillus of Lellis at San Giovanni Rotondo. Thus, the Monastery of Our Lady of Grace could be considered the remote birthplace of the Red Cross.

St. Camillus of Lellis was born in the Holy Year 1550, and he has the same birthday as Padre Pio, May 25.

Even before Camillus was born, his pious mother saw in a dream a little boy wearing on his breast a great red cross, and with his hand he was grasping a flag with the same sign; a multitude of young men with the same red cross was following the little boy. Later on, when Camillus of Lellis founded his Order dedicated to the service of the sick, he asked the

Supreme Pontiff for the privilege of being able to put on his Order's religious habit that red cross which his mother had once seen in a dream. The privilege was granted to him and from then on the Red Cross, as the distinctive sign of the Camillian Hospital Order, also became the symbol of Christian charity in general; thus, it was adopted later on by that worldwide institution so beneficial for all humanity, known to us as the Red Cross.

As we continue to leaf through the chronicle of the monastery, we are informed that at the beginning of the seventeenth century the little monastery church was completely renovated and somewhat enlarged, and in 1616 it was reconsecrated. Since that time it has not undergone further modification, and nowadays we can still admire it under its old appearance, although it had to yield to the great new church that emerged from its side in 1959.

For some time the Monastery of San Giovanni Rotondo served as a novitiate.

For the entire nineteenth century, the Monastery of Our Lady of Grace had to suffer from various suppressions: it was closed for the first time in 1811 and then reopened in 1816. Then came its suppression by the Italians, which caused it to be closed again in 1867. Some years later the Capuchin friars opened it once more, but it was quickly declared a shelter for beggars, and as a result, the brethren had to abandon it once more, in 1885. Yet another twenty-four years went by in this business of suppressions.

In August of 1909, the Capuchin friars were finally able to return to their monastery, but owing to their extreme poverty and that of the population, it would have taken many years before the monastery—which had been reduced to an uninhabitable state during the brothers' long absence—could once more become a worthy home for religious. In 1916, when Padre Pio went to San Giovanni Rotondo, the monastery was in a state of extreme misery.

The date of Padre Pio's arrival at San Giovanni Rotondo, July 22, 1916, undoubtedly signaled the beginning of a new era for the Monastery of Our Lady of Grace. The extraordinary way in which this monastery flourished has an intimate connection with Padre Pio's life and forms part of that copious harvest of works that arose out of Padre Pio's sufferings and sacrifices.

How many pages would have to be written about this new era by the old friar-chronicler, who passed on to us the humble history of the origin of San Giovanni Rotondo's monastery! How amazed would he be to see his old monastery, once buried in solitude, now great and imposing, the destination of countless pilgrims that nobody ever called, although many claim to have heard there an invitation too strong for them to resist.

With the year 1939, a new chapter begins in Padre Pio's life and consequently in that of his monastery as well. The time of great trials, which had begun in the years 1923-24, with the particular restrictions, had come to an end. Padre Pio came to be restored to public life and from then on he could easily dedicate himself to his mission. Thus, in 1940 the great projects of social works were born, but their immediate enactment was impeded by the war.

During this war there was yet more talk of a prodigy: San Giovanni Rotondo did not experience the travail of any attacks by air, nor did it undergo any damage! Over here, the War seemed to be distant, although in reality it was a heartbeat away; in fact, there was an airfield near the city of Foggia, which became a target, together with its outskirts, and was almost completely destroyed. San Giovanni Rotondo, on the other hand, remained miraculously unharmed.

"We have Padre Pio," the people of San Giovanni Rotondo said. "We're not afraid. In the vicinity of Padre Pio there is salvation!"

The postwar period eventually led to the fulfillment of the projected works. The old chronicler who passed on to us the account of Providence's first miracle, which occurred in 1548, would have quite a job to do now if he were to describe all the miracles of Providence proved to have occurred each day in his poor monastery ever since Padre Pio began his works. Of course, in the chronicle he would have given prominence to the gesture of that emigrant who was born in the Gargano region, went on to become an important figure in faraway America and used his fortune to give Padre Pio assistance of the utmost generosity. That assistance allowed the construction not of a little hospital but of a magnificent work, which we admire today in the House for the Relief of Suffering, a stone's throw away from the monastery. Who knows how many beautiful things the good friar chronicler could have written about the new life of his monastery, transformed by the life of his humble fellow brother, Padre Pio, and how carefully he would have exhorted us to see in this entire prodigy only God's loving work!

SOME IMPORTANT DATES

There are, finally, some dates to remember. They are feast days for Padre Pio and therefore also for his monastery, luminous stages of a long and tiring journey. The first of these memorable dates is January 22, 1953, the day Padre Pio celebrated his Golden Anniversary as a religious in the Capuchin Order, in the old little Church of Our Lady of Grace. It was an intimate and moving celebration, in which very many of Padre Pio's spiritual children participated.

Then came May 5, 1956—Padre Pio's patron Saint's day—with the grandiose inauguration of the House for the Relief of Suffering, celebrated by Cardinal Lercaro before ecclesiastical and civil authorities and a multitude of Padre Pio's devotees and spiritual children.

Here too, in this new church, on August 10, 1960, Padre Pio celebrated his Golden Anniversary as a priest. It was a great celebration, not only for Padre Pio but also for his monastery, for his Order and for all his spiritual children spread throughout the world. It was a feast of joy and thanksgiving that found its worthy conclusion in the solemn *Te Deum* of the evening Benediction, celebrated by Padre Pio.

The humble monastery, which sprang up from a little vineyard long unknown to the world, is now a highly luminous lighthouse, pointing out the good way of Christ's message to a human race tormented by a thousand troubles and fears. Since then, innumerable have been the souls who have found here—and still find—faith, along with its gifts and benefits! Truly, its original founders could not have been able to give this monastery and its church a name more beautiful and appropriate than "Our Lady of Grace"!

Chapter 19

THREE PLACES OF PILGRIMAGE

SAN GIOVANNI ROTONDO

The village of San Giovanni Rotondo, which is about ten minutes by car from Our Lady of Grace Monastery, and the hotels located throughout the vicinity of the monastery offer no attraction for visitors. Yet a little pilgrimage to the original church after which the area is named, and a stop at the cemetery where Padre Pio's parents rest, may well complete our visit.

The site where the area of San Giovanni Rotondo is now located was already known in pagan antiquity as a place of "religious worship." The foundation of the village, however, dates from the eleventh century. Between 1007 and 1095, the first habitations arose around a little temple once dedicated to Janus, that Roman divinity which had two faces, one looking at the past and the other at the future. This little temple was never destroyed, but became the first church in the area and was dedicated to St. John the Baptist, the veneration of whom was spread by the monks of a nearby monastery in the Gargano Mountains known as "San Giovanni in Lamis." This original church, which still exists today, gave the area of

San Giovanni its name; the adjective "Rotondo" is due to the round form of the ancient little pagan temple, which was never modified.

A local poet, Giovanni Scarale, eulogized this original little church in the following bit of verse:

SAINT JOHN FROM AFAR

Like a little pumpkin it seems to me,
Although an ancient church it be,
It has, as well, a friendly air,
All simplicity is there.

You'll see, if you look through the door,
A little altar, nothing more
Except perhaps a scattered chair,
That might belong just anywhere.

So dark, so dark within's the sight,
That owing to the lack of light,
Those who look might feel a scare
That moves them to depart from there.

And yet if only you would stay
To tarry somewhat on your way,
Before long, you should have to share
A joy inside beyond compare.

From that whitish thing, discolored
By the moisture, and open air
And one more thing: the beautiful
Simplicity, abandoned there.

Not far from this original little church is the cemetery of San Giovanni Rotondo. Even from the village it is possible to see the tall cypress trees, which in a double line transverse the entire cemetery in the form of an immense cross. The cemetery descends from the slope of the mountain towards the plains. Here we come across the local women at every hour. Clothed in black and wrapped in their great woolen shawls, they make their way slowly from tomb to tomb. They speak to nobody and greet nobody. They just pray. Fingering the beads with their hands, they recite Rosaries and requiems. Many of the women make this devout visit every day.

At the entrance to the cemetery, there is a crucifix which they greet first. Near the crucifix there is an iron ring with which, after bowing devoutly before the crucifix, they gently knock on the door. I once asked a peasant woman why she did so. She answered, "We don't go into a house without knocking first; and thus we also knock before entering the cemetery, which is the house of the dead." Another time, a woman from the village told me as she entered the cemetery, "We are only poor pilgrims here on earth. Our real home is up there in Heaven!" Then, with a glance and a wave of the hand, she pointed to the blue sky above, far from the dark green of the cypress trees.

Directly to our left as we enter the cemetery is the chapel of the Capuchin Fathers. Here lie Padre Pio's parents. Before their tombs there are always fresh flowers and many lighted candles from the faithful of the entire world who have spent time here in devout prayer.

Also in this cemetery is the tomb of Italia Betti, a former Communist converted to the Faith by Padre Pio. This highly intelligent mathematics instructor came from a very poor family. Her father was originally from Romagna and her mother from Padua. They emigrated to Brazil, where twelve of their thirteen children were born. Italia grew up in this family, in which all were Communists except for her pious sister Emerita, who by prayer brought the entire family back to the Faith—Italia and her mother coming back first.

Emerita led her mother to Padre Pio when Italia was already seriously ill, after she had literally been consumed in the fervor of her Communist ideal. It was not easy for Italia to follow her pious sister's advice, but later, once Italia had gone together with her mother to see Padre Pio, the road to conversion was not long. Italia herself, in her spiritual legacy written on August 15, 1950, Feast of the Assumption, says so:

> A few days were enough for me to understand in depth that the true life is not the one I had lived up to that point, to understand that certain moral principles in which I had been educated literally needed to be turned upside down, to understand beyond any question that it is absurd for men, who are but little, organized particles of the universe, to be the coordinating elements of all human discipline.

Man is a creature of God, yet he must realize that he is a part and not the whole; he must be aware that he is a little force that at every instant needs a guide in order to proceed.

And God did in fact become man to make us better understand; Jesus, with his continual example of supernaturality and above all by His death on the Cross, has taught us what doctrine of life we are to follow. No other doctrine can compare with it.

Italia Betti remained at San Giovanni Rotondo for the short time that was still granted her to live, offering prayers and sufferings for the return to faith in Christ of those with whom she had once fought against this same faith. She also offered up her own life, dying like a Saint.

Her tomb is on the right as we enter the cemetery. On the large marble plate that covers it, we read the following words from Sacred Scripture:

Et quasi Meridianus
Fulgor consurget Tibi.

(And like the midday splendor
Shall she arise unto Thee.)

MONTE SANT'ANGELO

Fifteen centuries ago, on May 8, 493, according to a tradition, St. Michael the Archangel appeared in a cave of the Gargano mountains. The sacred grotto of the apparition quickly became a shrine, around which a little city arose known as Monte Sant'Angelo, which owes its distinction precisely to this favor of St. Michael.

This unique shrine in the mountain, which may be reached by climbing up a wide eighty-nine step staircase sculpted in wood, was the destination of devout pilgrimages from the beginning. However, it reached the peak of its fame in the eighth century, becoming Italy's most important place of pilgrimage, especially during the Middle Ages. At that time, emperors, kings and princes from all over Europe, as well as pontiffs and Saints, came here on pilgrimages of penance or supplication in times of perils or calamities, or to fulfill their vows of thanksgiving for favors received.

No worldly power has ever been able to stop this continual flow to the Shrine of St. Michael which, like a fortress of faith, has resisted all the pressures of time, always remaining a secure refuge in every calamity and the greatest center of devotion to St. Michael. For years, the masses of pilgrims from all over the world have been joined by Padre Pio's innumerable devotees. Almost everybody who made a visit to Padre Pio later made an additional visit to the Shrine of St. Michael.

The shrine is located at a slightly higher altitude— 843 meters above sea level—and is about twenty kilometers, or twelve miles, from San Giovanni Rotondo and may easily be reached by the fine highways that lead right up to the shrine. Thus, even the briefest stay at San Giovanni Rotondo easily makes it possible to make this devotional visit to St. Michael and to one of the most ancient and celebrated shrines of the world.

ST. NICHOLAS OF BARI

A visit to Bari does not require much time; the distance from San Giovanni Rotondo is about eighty miles. From Foggia to Bari, it is an hour and a half by train. People going by car can use the excellent highways that go from San Giovanni Rotondo to the important center of Puglia, which, with its magnificent Shrine of St. Nicholas, unquestionably deserves a visit from us. In fact, quite a few of the faithful who go to San Giovanni Rotondo also include in their itinerary a visit to the Basilica of the Saint of Bari.

This city on the Adriatic Sea has always looked towards the Near East. Its very first ships sailed towards the eastern coasts, and from the earliest times its port has welcomed navigators coming from the East.

Here is where countless pilgrims began their pilgrimages to the Holy Land, and still begin them today. Masses of the faithful from the Near East have also come here on their way to the Holy City of Rome.

It should not be surprising, then, if a fourth century Bishop, a native of Asia Minor, on his journey to Rome arrived here at Bari, which was destined to become his city.

Saint Nicholas, Archbishop of Myra, went through Bari around the year 320 and, according to a tradition, predicted that one day he would return to Bari and remain there for good.

The fame of his holiness and many prodigies and miracles worked either during his life or after his death had a vast resonance in the East—especially in Asia Minor and Russia—and in the Catholic West. The city of Bari, however, had the privilege of receiving the Saint's precious relics into its custody.

St. Nicholas died in his own homeland towards the end of the fourth century, and his remains were laid in the Cathedral of Myra. However, seven centuries later, when the city of Myra fell into Saracen hands, some courageous sailors from Bari decided to embark on a journey to the East to salvage the Saint's remains and bring them back to their own city. The bold undertaking was successful, and on May 9, 1087, the ship pulled into the port of Bari, along with its precious cargo. Before long the people of Bari built in the Saint's honor that splendid shrine that we still admire today.

This shrine—like the city itself—has never looked away from the Near East; the destiny of the Eastern Church is intimately connected with it. Here the sorrowful division came, and here there has always been prayer—and always will be prayer—for the return to union. In the silence of the crypt, near the glorious tomb of the holy Bishop of Myra, fervent souls from East and West meet, and their prayers unite. Here, there has always been prayer for Russia as well: in the past, when her children still called her "Holy Russia," and now in our time, when the message of Fatima moves us to ask for the miracle of her conversion.

Our pilgrimage to Bari, then, may also be a pilgrimage for Russia, which in the past had a very special devotion for our Saint. How many pilgrims from faraway Russia and the Slavic countries used to come to Bari to venerate the tomb of St. Nicholas! Let us pray for those who have had to interrupt their pilgrimages, so that one day they may be able to resume them. Let us pray that all the fervent souls of the world may once again be able to live their little lives in the joy of full freedom to worship. Let us recommend to St. Nicholas here this great prayer, which countless human hearts would like to see answered.

In this shrine run by the Dominican Fathers, there is also the precious "Manna of St. Nicholas." It is a limpid and pure liquid that for many centuries has fallen drop by drop in a miraculous way from the relics of St. Nicholas. It is a gift that St. Nicholas still offers his devotees today, bestowing health to the sick and all sorts of favors in our necessities, through the devout use of this manna.

Chapter 20

IN CONCLUSION

At the end of this book, our devout thoughts go out to Padre Pio. His example and his inspired words, as well as his prayers and sacrifices in his religious and priestly life, have given limitless benefits to me and to a multitude of souls, in return for which we can do nothing less than acknowledge them and be grateful.

May this book be a sign of gratitude as well. I wrote it in the hope that it might contribute to making the true message of Padre Pio better known and appreciated. That message is a powerful call to the true values of life and a summons to us all to conduct ourselves in the love of Holy Church, our sure guide on the way of Christ, the only one that can make us happy even on this earth.

Naples
On the Feast of the Stigmata
of St. Francis of Assisi
September 17, 1964

EPILOGUE

In the very early hours of September 23, 1968, Padre Pio left us forever. For those of us who respected him greatly and loved him as our spiritual father, he left us too soon. We knew he suffered enormously, but after all those years we grew accustomed to seeing him so weak and yet so strong at the same time. Therefore, nobody was actually prepared for his death, not even his fellow brothers at the monastery.

When we look over his whole life—last years, last days, last hours—what we see is a life full and rich, where nothing was wanting. And his death too was a graceful transition to eternity.

In his last years, Padre Pio became weaker and weaker, but his interior strength grew proportionately; because of this strength, he was able to work till almost the last hour of his life, in spite of his physical sufferings. In this last period of his life, as they pushed him around in a wheelchair to bless us, this supernatural strength radiated from him as never before and strengthened us to an incredible degree.

The last three days of his life were his days of triumph, joy and fulfillment, even though they cost him a superhuman effort. In these glorious days, there came from all over the world to San Giovanni Rotondo many thousands of spiritual children of

Padre Pio. These were days of strenuous prayers for him; in fact, it was a solemn thanksgiving triduum which, without our realizing it, was to be the finale of his life.

The first day of this triduum was Friday, September 20, 1968. It was the fiftieth anniversary of Padre Pio's receiving the stigmata. September 20, 1918, was also a Friday, but how different was that Friday of fifty years earlier. How different was the village of San Giovanni Rotondo with its small, poor, unknown little monastery.

On that day Padre Pio was alone in the monastery. It was the vigil of St. Matthew the Apostle, and all the brothers went to a nearby village of San Marco in Lamis, where there is a famous church dedicated to this Apostle and Evangelist. It must have been God's providence that arranged this to be a day of solitude, silence and detachment. Extraordinary was the manner in which he was to meet Christ Crucified. Christ wanted to draw him to Himself forever. It was a day of capitulation, superhuman pain and an irreversible union with the Crucified. It was a sorrowful Friday.

All his life Padre Pio understood his priesthood and the priesthood in general as a co-crucifixion with Christ, and from this union with Christ he drew all his strength and graces for himself and others. A priest once complained to Padre Pio of the great suffering caused to him by human slander. Padre Pio answered, "Don't you know that we priests must be crucified together with Christ?"

September 20, 1968, was a day when Padre Pio

harvested the fruits of his priestly life, so full in sacrifices. Surrounded by thousands of his spiritual children, he could celebrate his thanksgiving sacrifice in
a new, large monastery church, brightly lit and decorated with hundreds of red roses. Padre Pio was visibly moved when he celebrated this Holy Mass, and
for all of us it was a most sacred moment. We were
filled with gratitude that Padre Pio had made it to
this day and that we were able to be here with him.

The following day was a day of rest, recollection
and silent prayer. Padre Pio came down in the late
afternoon to pray for an hour in the choir as usual
and to bless us.

Then came Sunday, the last day of his life. It did
not seem to be different from any other day, which
was full of sacrifices. On the contrary, we can say that
this last Sunday, September 22—compared to other
days and Sundays—demanded even greater sacrifices
and energy, for that was the day of the big get-
together of Padre Pio's spiritual children and the
prayer groups founded by him.

Tens of thousands of us came that day. Many
groups from Italy mainly, because in almost all Italian towns there are such groups, led by priests who
perform and support this apostolate of prayer, just as
Padre Pio designed it. God's providence arranged it
in such a manner that this biggest meeting of Padre
Pio's spiritual children took place on the last day of
his life.

Padre Pio loved his spiritual children. He had an
extraordinary gift of being able to reach them, no

matter how many there were, and help them when they needed it. He was a careful father to each of us, and whenever we needed help and strength, we got it from him. So it was only natural that we came in such numbers on this Sunday, which against anybody's guess, proved to be a farewell Sunday. We filled the church to bursting to attend his Holy Mass. The church and the altar were still decorated with red roses from the previous Friday. The church was solemnly lit, and once again our Padre Pio approached the altar to celebrate Holy Mass, which was his lifelong consolation and strength, and through which he obtained many graces and prayers for us.

We could see Padre Pio was very exhausted. It must have been a great sacrifice for him to come to the church at five o'clock in the morning to celebrate Mass. Surely he did it out of love for his spiritual children, yet it stretched his last remnants of strength to the limit. As always, his Holy Mass was very touching. It was as if he was disappearing in it. He gave First Holy Communion to two children, a boy and a girl. Then, at the end of Mass, something happened that had never happened before: Padre Pio fainted! A Capuchin standing next to him caught him and held him on his feet. Padre Pio was totally exhausted. This was his *Consummatum Est*—"It is finished!"

After several hours, he recovered sufficiently to be able to hear the confessions of the men who were on the waiting list. In the afternoon, he came into the choir loft to pray and remained there until the

evening devotions were finished. It was a long one—
the Rosary, sung litanies, Benediction and the
evening Mass. After the last tones sounded, Padre Pio
got up to give the usual blessing. But he could not
hold his arm up. One of his brother monks had to
help him hold his arm up, and so Padre Pio did bless
us. Three times he made the Sign of the Cross over
us. It was his last blessing.

* * *

Some hours later, around midnight, he called his
brother, Padre Pellegrino. He asked him what time
it was and if there were any stars in the sky. He also
asked if he had celebrated Holy Mass yet, and when
Padre Pellegrino replied he had not, Padre Pio said,
"Tomorrow morning you will celebrate Holy Mass for
me." Padre Pellegrino then granted his wish to be
taken outside onto the terrace, but Padre Pio immediately wanted to go back into his cell. He had difficulty breathing, and as it worsened, he said to Padre
Pellegrino, "If the Lord God calls me to Himself this
night, then please beg the brothers for their forgive-
ness for all the worries I have caused them." He also
asked that the superiors bless his spiritual children in
his name. Then he wanted to make a Confession.
Padre Pellegrino offered to call his confessor, but
Padre Pio said, "Do not disturb him. I'll confess to
you." Afterwards, he asked Padre Pellegrino to
repeat with him the renewal of his religious vows.
After this was completed, his condition greatly deteriorated. Padre Pellegrino called the brothers and

sent for the doctor. But in the meantime, Padre Pio breathed his last, without the death agony, and sweetly and easily as a child. The only words he repeated several times until the end were, "*Jesu . . . Maria . . . Jesu . . . Maria . . .*"

* * *

The following days were days of deep mourning. Padre Pio's body was laid out in the monastery church from Monday, September 23, till Thursday, September 26. Tens of thousands of people gathered to say goodbye to him. The church was opened twenty-four hours a day and Holy Masses were offered continuously because many priests came and took turns at the altars. People prayed fervently. For three nights they kept vigils at his body till the morning. We had much to be thankful for. Who can weigh how much he helped us with his prayers and life full of sacrifices?

On Friday, September 27, 1968, Padre Pio's body was laid to rest in the crypt beneath the main altar of the Monastery Church of Our Lady of Grace in San Giovanni Rotondo.

There are always many people praying in the silent crypt. The tomb of Padre Pio is a place of recollection and prayer. During his life, Padre Pio drew to himself first of all the suffering, the depressed and those seeking help, in order to alleviate their pain and to strengthen, encourage and help them. Today his tomb is a refuge for those who seek a home and who beg for help. The grateful ones are not lacking either. They have received his help and intercession.

Not everybody is fortunate enough to be able to visit Padre Pio's tomb. But wherever we might be, we can all reach him in prayer.

So we can ask in prayer that he remain close to us with his intercession, that he remain our father, who looks over us and helps us in our anxieties.

May he obtain for all of us—to whom he showed the way to Christ and love of God through his example, prayer and sacrifice, his admonitions and encouragement—the grace to walk through our lives faithfully, full of joy and gratefulness.

AMEN

Addendum

Padre Pio was beatified on May 2, 1999 by Pope John Paul II and canonized on June 16, 2002 by the same Pope.

For those wishing to correspond with Padre Pio's monastery, we give here the address of the Capuchin Monastery of San Giovanni Rotondo:

> Convento Cappuccini
> Santa Maria delle Grazie
> 1-71913 San Giovanni Rotondo
> Foggia. ITALY

Appendix

ABOUT THE AUTHOR

Katharina Tangari was born Anna Maria Augusta Katharina Hausslinger on March 10, 1906, in Vienna, Austria, of a very devout Catholic family. She was raised in a home centered on devotion to the Sacred Heart of Jesus, a devotion which her father instilled into the hearts of all his children.

A woman of great holiness, intelligence and culture, Katharina spoke seven languages, translated *The History of Italian Literature* by Papini into German for an Austrian publishing house, studied medicine and prepared forty scientific studies which would be published under the name of her husband, Corrado Tangari.

In 1936, at the age of thirty, Katharina moved to Naples, Italy, where she met and married Corrado Tangari, an Italian doctor. On her wedding day, August 16, 1943, at the Nuptial Mass, Katharina offered herself as a victim soul to the Sacred Heart of Jesus for the sanctification of married life.

Three months after her wedding day, the Austrian-born and German-speaking Madame Tangari was denounced as a spy and was arrested by Allied troops in Italy. (This was during World War II.) She was condemned to death by a military tribunal, but she argued in her own defense for nine hours, and her sentence was changed from death to imprisonment for the duration of the War. Thus, she spent the next three years of her life in prison camps, first at Padula, then at Terni and finally at Riccione, until she was eventually released at the end of the War on October 12, 1946.

After the War, Madame Tangari and her husband moved to Vienna, Austria. There, Madame Tangari's husband deserted her and moved back to Naples. Feeling her duty was to be near her husband, she too moved back to Naples; while there, she would call her husband on the telephone to ask his permission each time she wished to leave town.

Madame Tangari first heard about Padre Pio in 1949 while making a pilgrimage to the Shrine of St. Nicholas at Bari in the south of Italy. The following year she met Padre Pio for the first time and became his spiritual daughter. For the next eighteen years, Padre Pio was Madame Tangari's spiritual director, until his death in 1968.

During the course of her life, Madame Tangari made regular pilgrimages to various shrines, including Mariazell, the Shrine of the Infant Jesus of Prague, Altotting, Lourdes, Fatima, Pompeii, Scala Santa and Sainte Marie in Cosmodine. Once, in 1951, after having paid a visit to her family in Vienna, Madame Tangari was on her way to the famous Shrine of Our Lady of Mariazell, the protectress of Austria. At that time, Austria was still partly occupied by Soviet forces, and to reach this shrine, one had to go through the Russian Sector.

Madame Tangari was traveling by bus with some other pilgrims, and when they reached a certain checkpoint, they were asked to show their passports to the officers. After showing her passport, Madame Tangari was taken off the bus. She remembered hearing that if someone were taken off the bus and brought into the checkpoint, that person usually would never be seen again. Her luggage was also taken off, and the bus with the other pilgrims went on without her.

As the officers dragged her towards the door of the office, Madame Tangari vowed to Our Lady that if she were spared, she would make a pilgrimage each year, walking barefoot from that point to the shrine at Mariazell.

When they reached the door of the office, Madame Tangari became immovable. The officers tried everything to move her, but could not do so, even after three full hours.

At midday the guards changed, and at that moment Madame Tangari noticed a man standing in some trees a short distance from her. The man shouted to her, "Run! Now!" and Madame Tangari ran towards this man, who led her for hours through the woods until they finally came to the great Basilica of Mariazell.

Madame Tangari entered the church and knelt down at the altar rail to thank Our Lady for delivering her from the hands of the Russians. It was now about five o'clock in the afternoon. A priest then came out of the sacristy, vested in a stole and a surplice. He walked up to her and said, "You're the lady who requested Holy Communion, aren't you?"

After receiving Holy Communion and making her thanksgiving, Madame Tangari went to the hotel where she had made reservations. As she entered the hotel, the receptionist at the desk said to her, "Oh, yes, Madame Tangari! Your luggage has just been delivered!" As she had promised to do, Madame Tangari faithfully made her thanksgiving pilgrimage to the Shrine of the Virgin of Mariazell on the first Saturday of November each year from 1951 until 1988 (the year before her death), except when she was in prison. She made this pilgrimage barefoot, walking from the place she had been miraculously set free all the way to the shrine, which was about four and a half miles away.

Though she had been delivered that day from Soviet troops, she would soon begin an apostolate that would bring her even closer to the threat of the Communists. In 1964, Padre Pio announced to her that she was to go to Prague in Czechoslovakia with suitcases full of scapulars, rosaries, medals and other sacramentals, which she was to obtain by begging money from her friends and relatives. At first Madame Tangari protested, saying, "Father, they put you in jail for doing those things!" But Padre Pio insisted, saying, "Well, you go home and pray about it, because that is God's will for you."

Thus, under the direction of Padre Pio, Madame

Tangari began her extraordinary apostolate of bringing religious items, medicines and other needed things to persecuted Catholics, especially to priests, behind the Iron Curtain. Between 1964 and 1971 she made over 100 journeys to Poland, Czechoslovakia and Hungary, crossing the Communist borders with as many as seven or eight suitcases filled with religious items and other needed things.

There are many stories about these journeys that illustrate God's special protection of Madame Tangari in her apostolate. We are told, for example, that when her train would reach its checkpoints, Madame Tangari would kneel down and pray the Rosary. When the guards came to check her compartment, they would look around and move on to the next compartment as though they had not even seen Madame Tangari.

Through all the years of this apostolate, Madame Tangari never once wrote down an address, but kept all the necessary addresses in her head so that she would never be the cause of anybody being betrayed or any of these houses being closed down.

After Padre Pio's death in 1968, Madame Tangari continued her active ministry. During this time she brought several copies of her book about Padre Pio with her to Czechoslovakia. There, someone translated it into Czech, printed it surreptitiously and began to distribute it—leaving Madame Tangari's name on it as the author. Because of this, Madame Tangari was denounced to the authorities, and on April 15, 1971, while waiting at the border of

Czechoslovakia, she was arrested and put into solitary confinement in a prison in Bratislava.

During her first interrogations at Bratislava, Madame Tangari denied everything she was accused of. We are told that when she returned to her cell, she heard the voice of Padre Pio, who had been dead for three years, saying, "A pack of lies! A pack of lies! A pack of lies!" And she answered, "Well, Padre Pio, if you want me to tell the truth, you better arrange it so that I can do so!"

Madame Tangari said that from that point until she was released fifteen months later, any question put to her was put in such a manner that she could truthfully give an answer without telling a lie and without denouncing or betraying any of the people she had helped.

From Bratislava Madame Tangari was moved to the infamous prison in Prague. There she remained for the last eleven months of her sentence, suffering continuous interrogations and torture. She shared a thirteen-square-foot cell with twelve or thirteen other women. In the center of the cell was a low cement block around which the women had to sleep, leaning against each other's backs. For their waste there was a bucket in the corner of the room. During the day they could not sit down, nor could they sleep. The light was on twenty-four hours a day, and the food they were given was pitiful. Near the end of her imprisonment, Madame Tangari's skin began to turn black from malnutrition.

At her trial, Madame Tangari had been charged

with "spreading seditious literature" and sentenced to fifteen months' imprisonment. When she returned to her cell after the trial, she wondered at her sentence. Why fifteen months? We are told that at this moment Our Lady appeared to her and said, "It is because you are a lover of the Rosary!" and then disappeared. Madame Tangari understood that the fifteen months symbolized the fifteen decades of the Rosary.

The story of this apparition was related by Madame Tangari on the Sunday before her death. It was told to a young boy who had just received his First Holy Communion. This boy had heard his parents speak of Madame Tangari as a saintly woman who was very close to Our Lady. In all innocence and simplicity, the boy asked her on her sick bed, "Have you ever seen Our Lady?" and she recounted this incident to him.

After serving her fifteen-month sentence, Madame Tangari returned home on July 6, 1972, knowing that she could never again return to the countries behind the Iron Curtain. But since she could no longer help priests and Catholics persecuted in the East, she began an apostolate to help priests persecuted in the West who were trying to preserve the traditional Roman rite of the Mass. From 1974 until her death fifteen years later, Madame Tangari undertook an enormous liturgical apostolate, providing traditional chapels with all the things necessary for celebrating Mass in the traditional Roman rite: chalices, ciboria, monstrances, ornaments, candlesticks, etc. Madame Tangari herself lived in great poverty, but she entrusted everything to Divine Providence, whom she would beg and to whom she would offer her physical sufferings for the continuance of her work, and donations would arrive from throughout Europe to support her liturgical apostolate.

Towards the end of 1988, Madame Tangari's health began to fail her. She became especially ill after receiving a new identification card, on which was written for the first time: "Marital Status: Divorced"! She was devastated at being considered a divorced woman after so many years of being faithful to her husband.

By January of 1989, Madame Tangari could no longer take care of herself. Her health had deteriorated very quickly. Just one year earlier, at the age of eighty, she had made a pilgrimage to Fatima, where she made the Stations of the Cross on her knees and prayed the fifteen decades of the Rosary with outstretched arms! Now she was dependent upon others for her most basic needs.

She was taken into a house of the Society of St. Pius X at Albano, Italy, where she would spend the last ten months of her life. While there, she prayed that she might have her Purgatory here on earth. A short time later, her blood pressure went up to 260 and she became blind. Then, on July 14, she fell and cracked her hip, but she was unable to be operated on for a couple days, until her blood pressure could be brought down. After surgery on her hip, she could hardly walk at all. But through it all, she kept her spirit of patience, humility and faith. When asked by a visiting priest what advice she could give him in his work, her reply was, "Put souls in the presence of God!"

Her health gradually worsened through November of that same year. Then, during the afternoon of December 1, 1989, the First Friday of the month, her death agony began. For three hours Madame Tangari offered herself up to the Sacred Heart of Jesus and begged Our Lord for the glorification of Padre Pio. She died at 5:00 p.m. that afternoon.

Crowds of people came to pay their last respects, touching various articles to her hands. She was buried in the habit of a Dominican tertiary (she had become a third order Dominican in 1950) and was laid to rest in Zaitzkoffen, Germany, on the Feast of St. Nicholas, the Saint to whose shrine she had been on pilgrimage when she first heard about Padre Pio.

Looking back on her eighteen years under Padre Pio's spiritual direction, Madame Tangari once explained that those years had been divided into three periods, each with its own message for spiritual growth. During the first period, Padre Pio had taught Madame Tangari to have a special devotion to the most holy Rosary. He would say to her, "In all the free time you have, once you have finished your duties of state, you should kneel down and pray the Rosary. Pray the Rosary before the Blessed Sacrament or before a Crucifix." During the second period, he taught her to possess her soul in peace. And during the third period, from about 1962 onwards, he taught her very emphatically the importance of thanking God for everything that happens. After one confession, on May 3, 1965, the following discourse took place:

"You must thank God for everything that happens to you in life!" Padre Pio said to Madame Tangari. "Do you understand?"

"Yes, Father, I understand."

Repeating himself, Padre Pio said, "Really, you must thank God always, for no matter what happens to you in life! Do you understand?"

"Yes, Father," she said again, "I understand."

For a third time he repeated, "You must thank God always for whatever happens to you in life! Do you understand?"

Again she answered, "Yes, Father, I understand."

At that time she wondered at the insistence of Padre Pio in repeating this exhortation three times; but a few days later, on May 9, it became clear to her why he had done so.

While Madame Tangari was saying her thanksgiving prayers after Mass, some friends came to her and informed her that her house was burning down. She rushed back to her house and found it in an absolute rage of fire; but, standing near the blazing fire, she was heard to say, *"Deo Gratias!"*—*"Thanks be to God!"* Her friends thought she had gone mad.

After the fire had cooled down, Madame Tangari rustled through the rubble and, though all else was destroyed, she found three things which were totally untouched by the flames: The first was a statue of the

Infant Jesus of Prague, to whom she had a very special devotion; the second was a picture of Our Lady Immaculate; and the third was the manuscript of what she had written about Padre Pio (this present book). All the pages of this manuscript were completely untouched by the flames.

The following week Madame Tangari again approached Padre Pio for Confession. As she stood in line to await her turn to confess, Padre Pio walked by, turned to her and said, "Now do you understand that you must thank God for all that happens to you in life?" Madame Tangari said that from that moment she knew she had to live for God and for God alone!

And live for God she did. Each day, she assisted at one or more Masses, prayed the Rosary, the Office of the Blessed Virgin Mary and the Way of the Cross; each Friday she made a complete fast, not even allowing herself a glass of water, a practice which she continued even in prison.

Towards the end of her life, many believed that Madame Tangari had the power to read hearts. She was often consulted regarding religious vocations or future marriages. People would approach her, for example, and say, "My daughter is engaged to so-and-so. Could you please pray for them?" After praying for some days, Madame Tangari would return, saying, "Get rid of him! It will never work out! God will never bless this marriage!" Or she would say, "God will bless this marriage. It will be all right." Since her death, many have prayed to Madame Tangari for their needs, especially regarding vocational discernment and marital problems.

Before leaving this world, Madame Tangari prepared the following memento:

"Any good that I was able to do in my life was a pure grace of God, not merited. That you, thrice sweet Mother of God, have willed to give me so much love for you has been my complete recompense."

In publishing this book, it is our hope as publishers that a greater knowledge of and interest in Padre Pio, the subject of this work, might be spread, but at the same time that its author, Madame Katharina Tangari, might become better known as well.

Anthony J. Mioni, Editor
TAN Books and Publishers, Inc.
August 1, 1996

(Grateful acknowledgment to Father Emmanuel du Chalard and Father Gerard Hogan for material used in this Preface. Most of the material used was taken from the Preface to the French edition of this book, *Le Message De Padre Pio*, published by Courrier de Rome, and from *Madame Tangari*, a transcript of a talk given by the Rev. Fr. Gerard Hogan at the Catholic Resource Center, Mildura, Victoria on February 28, 1990.)

***If you have enjoyed this book, consider making your
next selection from among the following . . .***

Prices subject to change.

Prices subject to change.

Forty Dreams of St. John Bosco. *Bosco* 15.00
Blessed Miguel Pro. *Ball* 7.50
Soul Sanctified. *Anonymous* 12.00
Wife, Mother and Mystic. *Bessieres* 10.00
The Agony of Jesus. *Padre Pio* 3.00
Catholic Home Schooling. *Mary Kay Clark* 21.00
The Cath. Religion—Illus. & Expl. *Msgr. Burbach* 12.50
Wonders of the Holy Name. *Fr. O'Sullivan* 2.50
How Christ Said the First Mass. *Fr. Meagher* 21.00
Too Busy for God? Think Again! *D'Angelo* 7.00
St. Bernadette Soubirous. *Trochu* 21.00
Pope Pius VII. *Anderson* 16.50
Life Everlasting. *Garrigou-Lagrange* 16.50
Confession Quizzes. *Radio Replies Press* 2.50
St. Philip Neri. *Fr. V. J. Matthews* 7.50
St. Louise de Marillac. *Sr. Vincent Regnault* 7.50
The Old World and America. *Rev. Philip Furlong* 21.00
Prophecy for Today. *Edward Connor* 7.50
Bethlehem. *Fr. Faber* 20.00
The Book of Infinite Love. *Mother de la Touche* 7.50
The Church Teaches. *Church Documents* 18.00
Conversation with Christ. *Peter T. Rohrbach* 12.50
Purgatory and Heaven. *J. P. Arendzen* 6.00
Liberalism Is a Sin. *Sarda y Salvany* 9.00
Spiritual Legacy/Sr. Mary of Trinity. *van den Broek* .. 13.00
The Creator and the Creature. *Fr. Frederick Faber* ... 17.50
Radio Replies. 3 Vols. *Frs. Rumble and Carty* 48.00
Convert's Catechism of Catholic Doctrine. *Geiermann* .. 5.00
Incarnation, Birth, Infancy of Jesus Christ. *Liguori* . 13.50
Light and Peace. *Fr. R. P. Quadrupani* 8.00
Dogmatic Canons & Decrees of Trent, Vat. I 11.00
The Evolution Hoax Exposed. *A. N. Field* 9.00
The Priest, the Man of God. *St. Joseph Cafasso* 16.00
Christ Denied. *Fr. Paul Wickens* 3.50
New Regulations on Indulgences. *Fr. Winfrid Herbst* ... 3.00
A Tour of the Summa. *Msgr. Paul Glenn* 22.50
Spiritual Conferences. *Fr. Frederick Faber* 18.00
Bible Quizzes. *Radio Replies Press* 2.50
Marriage Quizzes. *Radio Replies Press* 2.50
True Church Quizzes. *Radio Replies Press* 2.50
Mary, Mother of the Church. *Church Documents* 5.00
The Sacred Heart and the Priesthood. *de la Touche* ... 10.00
Blessed Sacrament. *Fr. Faber* 20.00
Revelations of St. Bridget. *St. Bridget of Sweden* 4.50

Prices subject to change.

Story of a Soul. *St. Therese of Lisieux.* 9.00
Catholic Children's Treasure Box Books 1-10 . . . . 40.00
Prayers and Heavenly Promises. *Cruz.* 5.00
Magnificent Prayers. *St. Bridget of Sweden.* 2.00
The Happiness of Heaven. *Fr. J. Boudreau* 10.00
The Holy Eucharist—Our All. *Fr. Lucas Etlin* 3.00
The Glories of Mary. *St. Alphonsus Liguori* 21.00
The Curé D'Ars. *Abbé Francis Trochu* 24.00
Humility of Heart. *Fr. Cajetan da Bergamo* 9.00
Love, Peace and Joy. (St. Gertrude). *Prévot* 8.00
Père Lamy. *Biver* 15.00
Passion of Jesus & Its Hidden Meaning. *Groenings* 15.00
Mother of God & Her Glorious Feasts. *Fr. O'Laverty* 15.00
Song of Songs—A Mystical Exposition. *Fr. Arintero* 21.50
Love and Service of God, Infinite Love. *de la Touche* 15.00
Life & Work of Mother Louise Marg. *Fr. O'Connell.* 15.00
Martyrs of the Coliseum. *O'Reilly* 21.00
Rhine Flows into the Tiber. *Fr. Wiltgen* 16.50
What Catholics Believe. *Fr. Lawrence Lovasik* 6.00
Who Is Therese Neumann? *Fr. Charles Carty.* 3.50
Summa of the Christian Life. 3 Vols. *Granada* 43.00
St. Francis of Paola. *Simi and Segreti* 9.00
The Rosary in Action. *John Johnson.* 12.00
St. Dominic. *Sr. Mary Jean Dorcy* 13.50
Is It a Saint's Name? *Fr. William Dunne* 3.00
St. Martin de Porres. *Giuliana Cavallini* 15.00
Douay-Rheims New Testament. *Paperbound* 16.50
St. Catherine of Siena. *Alice Curtayne* 16.50
Blessed Virgin Mary. *Liguori* 7.50
Chats With Converts. *Fr. M. D. Forrest* 13.50
The Stigmata and Modern Science. *Fr. Charles Carty.* 2.50
St. Gertrude the Great 2.50
Thirty Favorite Novenas 1.50
Brief Life of Christ. *Fr. Rumble* 3.50
Catechism of Mental Prayer. *Msgr. Simler* 3.00
On Freemasonry. *Pope Leo XIII* 2.50
Thoughts of the Curé D'Ars. *St. John Vianney* 3.00
Incredible Creed of Jehovah Witnesses. *Fr. Rumble* 3.00
St. Pius V—His Life, Times, Miracles. *Anderson* 7.00
St. Dominic's Family. *Sr. Mary Jean Dorcy* 27.50
St. Rose of Lima. *Sr. Alphonsus* 16.50
Latin Grammar. *Scanlon & Scanlon* 18.00
Second Latin. *Scanlon & Scanlon.* 16.50
St. Joseph of Copertino. *Pastrovicchi* 8.00

Prices subject to change.

Holy Eucharist—Our All. *Fr. Lukas Etlin, O.S.B.* 3.00
Glories of Divine Grace. *Fr. Scheeben* 18.00
Saint Michael and the Angels. *Approved Sources* 9.00
Dolorous Passion of Our Lord. *Anne C. Emmerich* 18.00
Our Lady of Fatima's Peace Plan from Heaven. *Booklet* 1.00
Three Ways of the Spiritual Life. *Garrigou-Lagrange.* 7.00
Mystical Evolution. 2 Vols. *Fr. Arintero, O.P.* 42.00
St. Catherine Labouré of the Mirac. Medal. *Fr. Dirvin* 16.50
Manual of Practical Devotion to St. Joseph. *Patrignani.* 17.50
The Active Catholic. *Fr. Palau* 9.00
Ven. Jacinta Marto of Fatima. *Cirrincione* 3.00
Reign of Christ the King. *Davies* 2.00
St. Teresa of Avila. *William Thomas Walsh* 24.00
Isabella of Spain—The Last Crusader. *Wm. T. Walsh* 24.00
Characters of the Inquisition. *Wm. T. Walsh* 16.50
Blood-Drenched Altars—Cath. Comment. Hist. Mexico 21.50
Self-Abandonment to Divine Providence. *de Caussade.* 22.50
Way of the Cross. *Liguorian.* 1.50
Way of the Cross. *Franciscan.* 1.50
Modern Saints—Their Lives & Faces, Bk. 1. *Ann Ball* 21.00
Modern Saints—Their Lives & Faces, Bk. 2. *Ann Ball* 23.00
Divine Favors Granted to St. Joseph. *Pere Binet* 7.50
St. Joseph Cafasso—Priest of the Gallows. *St. J. Bosco* 6.00
Catechism of the Council of Trent. *McHugh/Callan* 27.50
Why Squander Illness? *Frs. Rumble & Carty* 4.00
Fatima—The Great Sign. *Francis Johnston.* 12.00
Heliotropium—Conformity of Human Will to Divine 15.00
Charity for the Suffering Souls. *Fr. John Nageleisen.* 18.00
Devotion to the Sacred Heart of Jesus. *Verheylezoon* 16.50
Sermons on Prayer. *St. Francis de Sales* 7.00
Sermons on Our Lady. *St. Francis de Sales.* 15.00
Sermons for Lent. *St. Francis de Sales* 15.00
Fundamentals of Catholic Dogma. *Ott* 27.50
Litany of the Blessed Virgin Mary. (100 cards) 5.00
Who Is Padre Pio? *Radio Replies Press* 3.00
Child's Bible History. *Knecht* 7.00
St. Anthony—The Wonder Worker of Padua. *Stoddard* 7.00
The Precious Blood. *Fr. Faber* 16.50
The Holy Shroud & Four Visions. *Fr. O'Connell* 3.50
Clean Love in Courtship. *Fr. Lawrence Lovasik* 4.50
The Secret of the Rosary. *St. Louis De Montfort.* 5.00

At your Bookdealer or direct from the Publisher.
Call Toll Free 1-800-437-5876

Prices subject to change.